DAVID SAMUEL BARR

President, Zachary Associates

ADVERTISING
ON
CABLE

A Practical Guide for Advertisers

PRENTICE-HALL, INC., *Englewood Cliffs, NJ 07632*

Library of Congress Cataloging in Publication Data

Barr, David Samuel (date)
  Advertising on cable.

  Includes indexes.
  1. Cable television advertising. I. Title.
HF6146.T42B36 1985   659.14′3   84-26548
ISBN 0-13-014531-9

Editorial/production supervision and interior design: Maureen Wilson
Cover design: Joe Curcio
Manufacturing buyer: Ed O'Dougherty

Printed in the United States of America

10 9 8 7 6 5 4 3 2 1

ISBN 0-13-014531-9   01

PRENTICE-HALL INTERNATIONAL, INC., *London*
PRENTICE-HALL OF AUSTRALIA PTY. LIMITED, *Sydney*
EDITORA PRENTICE-HALL DO BRASIL, LTDA., *Rio de Janeiro*
PRENTICE-HALL CANADA INC., *Toronto*
PRENTICE-HALL HISPANOAMERICANA, S.A., *Mexico*
PRENTICE-HALL OF INDIA PRIVATE LIMITED, *New Delhi*
PRENTICE-HALL OF JAPAN, INC., *Tokyo*
PRENTICE-HALL OF SOUTHEAST ASIA PTE. LTD., *Singapore*
WHITEHALL BOOKS LIMITED, *Wellington, New Zealand*

To my parents and sisters,
for their constant encouragement, constructive criticism,
and a little noodging now and then when necessary.

CONTENTS

FOREWORD

President, Cabletelevision Advertising Bureau

The most dramatic challenge facing any business that sells to the consumer today is market segmentation. Companies are coming to realize more and more that the route to future sales growth will depend on how well they adapt their marketing, merchandising, and advertising approaches to this growing phenomenon.

Market segmentation is a primary subject of discussion at many different industry trade meetings and in the business press. The consensus is that the splintering of mass markets is forcing companies to target their products and services. Thoughtful observers and practitioners of marketing and merchandising have come to the conclusion that a nation that once shared homogeneous buying tastes has splintered into many consumer groups, each with different needs and interests.

Companies like Procter & Gamble were built on the principles of mass marketing. Yet a study of P&G's recent new product development efforts reveals how strongly the segment marketing current is running. Most of these products are being aimed at special market segments. The realization, based on the type of consumer research they are so rightly famous for, has set in that we are at the end of the era of mass marketing.

General Foods acknowledges that although most of its products are universally consumed, the grocery market is divided into at least six subgroups, each of which will have to be approached differently, even for the same brand.

There is a seemingly endless proliferation of brands and variations in product formulation for soft drinks, cigarettes, automobiles, soap, bread, beer, and just about every consumer product category. Even those considered to be staples, where relatively few brands once dominated, are not immune.

Thus advertisers are looking for new ways to sell and to make their media dollars work harder. They want to reach their target groups more efficiently and with messages relevant to them.

The changes in the 1980s that have taken place in society and in the family are having a profound effect on marketing. Even with the current preoccupation with computers, the marketplace is being driven by the consumer, not by technology. Lifestyles and values, not more standard demographics, are growing in terms of primary importance.

Given these rapid changes in demographics and lifestyles, it has become inevitable that television, with which consumers spend more time and which is more responsive to taste and interest than any other product or service, could no longer resist this move to segmentation.

The three television networks cannot serve the tastes and needs of 230 million Americans. This fact is evidenced by the shifts in audience shares that have occurred with the development of the technology that allows the distribution of alternative programming via cable.

In the last four years, "Cable America" has increased in size from 20 million homes to 37 million—more than 43 percent of all television homes—with almost 50 percent of the nation's buying power. And cable homes are increasing at the rate of almost 400,000 every month.

People are watching this alternative programming. What does this diversification in viewing mean to people in advertising? For the first time, they have the opportunity to design television campaigns for specific markets—based on lifestyles, not just demographics. It opens up creative opportunities to make specific commercials for specific consumers—and in longer form, if needed to tell the product story.

Cable has changed forever the television viewing habits of America. Once viewers have experienced program choice, they are no longer satisfied with the limits of traditional broadcast television. The opportunities this opens up for the advertiser are as vast and varied as the audience.

In order for advertisers to take advantage of the sales-building opportunities cable offers, it is important that the unique qualities of the medium be understood. For this reason, I am extremely pleased that David undertook to write this book. He has managed to bring a pragmatic point of view to a complex subject that was, and is, in a constant state of change and development. It will serve as a very valuable resource for the many advertisers concerned that their media plans not only accommodate the rapid changes in the way people are watching television because of cable, but also the shifting buying patterns that have transformed marketing and merchandising in this country.

PREFACE

In my experience as manager of information services at the Cabletelevision Advertising Bureau (CAB) and in my own consulting business, I have dealt with hundreds of advertisers and agencies that have asked many different questions. Yet what each of those questions inevitably boiled down to was, "How do I use cable?"

This book is meant to answer that question by giving a comprehensive look at the various characteristics of cable and the opportunities it offers advertisers, together with numerous examples of how advertisers have used cable successfully on both a national and a local level. It is not an academic treatise on advertising theory (although it no doubt can be valuable as part of an advertising course), nor is it by any means a cable industry puff piece designed to sell cable, although I readily admit that after ten years in and around cable I do have a little pro-cable bias. Rather it is designed to be a practical marketing tool that advertisers can refer to on a regular basis for information and ideas, whether they are launching a major campaign for a multinational food company or announcing a high school bake sale.

The cable industry is a volatile one, and a standard rule of thumb is that anything written about it that is more than two weeks old is hopelessly out of date. I have tried to keep this book on a sufficiently generic level so that it will be useful for years to come. It is inevitable, though, that some individual details or statistics may have changed by the time you read this. Nevertheless, the concepts they illustrate remain valid. The real purpose of the examples used in the book is to start you thinking about how to adapt these ideas to your own benefit.

This book has been written from the standpoint of the hundreds of people in the cable industry and the advertising world who have been buying, selling, using, developing, and promoting cable advertising, and is by no means solely the product of my own work. Many of my colleagues were kind enough to take time out to share their experience and expertise with me, including Bill Adams, Susan S. Aron, Michael P. Ban, Irwin Barnett, William Behanna, Perry Black, Gregory Blaine, Frank Brady, Bob Caporeale, Larry Colbert, Katherine Connolly, Andrew Curcio, Brenda Davidorf, Larry Divney, Ed Dooley, Vess Duro, Mel Farber, John Fernandez, Robert Finehout, John Florescu, Annemarie Frisch, Chuck Fruit, Michael Fugatt, Sheldon Hechtman, Bruce R. Hoban, John Howard, Donna Inzinga, Bob Jeremiah, Charles Jones, Tom Keegan, Brian Kelly, Ray Klinge, Michael Koslow, Trevor Lambert, Jeffrey B. Lawenda, Richard Marshall, Glenn A. Northrop, Donald M. Olson, Connie Pettit, Farrell Reynolds, Mark Roffman, Fred Schwartzfarbe, Donna Sparks, Toby Steinberg, Janis Thomas, Robert Treuber, Terri Troja, Linda Watts, Robert Williams, and David Wolk. Many others supplied me with various clarifications, statistics, and artwork, often in response to frantic last-minute requests. My sincere thanks to all of them.

I would like to extend special thanks to the entire staff of CAB, particularly Lynne A. Nordone, Lela Cocoros, James B. Boyle, Richard Zackon, and Vincent J. Fazio, for their moral support, their generous assistance in gathering, verifying, and updating information, and especially their tolerance of my commandeering their computer for weeks at a time. Special thanks also to the people at Prentice-Hall: Ted Jursek, for suggesting this book in the first place; Dennis Hogan and Kathryn Pavelec, for patiently waiting for my usually overdue manuscripts; and Maureen Wilson and the rest of her production team who put a special effort into getting this book out in half the usual time.

Finally, a special word of gratitude to Robert H. Alter, president of CAB. When Ted Jursek originally asked him to write a book on cable advertising for Prentice-Hall, Bob invited me to co-author it with him. After we had worked on it for a while, though, Bob found that his schedule did not permit him to continue to participate fully in the writing process, and he graciously suggested that I finish the book myself and receive sole authorship credit. I cannot, though, let his valuable contributions go unrecognized. Bob not only read most of the chapters in their early stages and proposed revisions, but also provided essential structural suggestions for several chapters. There are even a number of sections in the book that he originally wrote, such as the "Setting Your Objectives" section of Chapter 3, which I have retained—pardon the pun—essentially unaltered.

ONE

THE DEVELOPMENT OF CABLE

Cable television began back in the late 1940s, in Oregon and Pennsylvania (the name of the person credited as the "father of cable" and the actual place of its birth varies depending on who is telling the story). At that time, and for the 25 years afterwards, the purpose of cable was to bring television signals into areas where they could be seen only poorly, if at all. During that period, the potential for expansion was hinted at as systems began to import broadcasts from television stations in distant cities in addition to the stations in their local markets, and in some cases to introduce local origination and public access channels that presented locally produced programs. It was with the development of satellite distribution of domestic television signals in the mid-1970s, combined with the trend toward building systems whose capacity exceeded the 12 channels on the VHF tuning dial on the standard television set, that cable truly took on a new role as an alternative entertainment supplier.

In 1975, Home Box Office became the first service to be made available by satellite on a national basis, and only to cable subscribers who paid an additional monthly fee to see the uncut current movies it offered. A competing network, Showtime, appeared the following year. Soon, people who didn't have significant reception problems, or who didn't watch television as a rule, were buying cable just to get the additional services.

As a result of the demand for new services by cable operators and subscribers alike, a plethora of new cable programming services sprang up in the late 1970s and early 1980s. During this time, some programmers began to realize that they could not expect cable subscribers to pay another $10 a month for every new service offered them. These programmers thought they could develop networks that would be advertiser-supported and offered to subscribers at no additional fee.[1] Soon, cable subscribers found that while they could subscribe to new pay services such as The Movie Channel, Cinemax, and GalaVision, their basic fee would also bring them such other networks as Cable News Network, ESPN, and Satellite Program Network, to name but a few.

BASIC/PAY CABLE SUBSCRIBER GROWTH

Year	Basic Subscribers	Percent of TVHHs	Pay Subscribers	Percent of TVHHs
1990	58,900,000	62%	43,700,000	46%
1989	54,988,000	59	40,076,000	43
1988	52,098,000	57	36,560,000	40
1987	49,280,000	55	33,152,000	37
1986	45,656,000	52	29,852,000	34
1985	40,467,000	47	25,830,000	30
1984	35,448,000	42	21,944,000	26
1983	30,636,000	37	18,216,000	22
1982	26,016,000	32	14,634,000	18
1981	22,596,000	28	11,804,000	14
1980	18,672,000	24	7,780,000	10
1979	16,023,000	21	5,341,000	7
1978	14,155,000	19	2,980,000	4
1977	13,194,000	18	1,466,000	2
1976	12,094,000	17	565,000	1

TVHHs = Television households.
Pay subscribers = Basic subscribers also subscribing to one or more pay cable services.
SOURCE: ICR, Cable Information Service—a Titsch Communications division.

[1]By that time, WTBS had already been running nationally for a few years as an advertiser-supported service, as had been several noncommercial religious programming networks that fed both cable systems and regular television stations by satellite, but these were seen more as additional distant broadcast television services than as cable services per se.

The American public has responded enthusiastically to cable's new offerings. Each day, approximately 400,000 households become cable subscribers. By the end of 1983, over 40 percent of all American television households had cable; that number is expected to reach 50 percent in 1985 and to exceed 60 percent by 1990. Ninety-three percent of all counties in the U.S. have some form of cable, and, contrary to popular belief that cable is still essentially a rural phenomenon, two-thirds of all cable subscribers are in A & B counties.[2]

Already, cable has not only changed the way America watches television, including creating a major decline in viewing of broadcast network offerings, it has changed the way America lives. The results of a study examining the impact of cable on household behavior, reported in the Advertising Research Foundation's *Journal of Advertising Research*, showed a trend toward a significant decrease in activities outside the home and time spent on other media, coupled with a sharp increase in in-home entertainment and family contact.

IMPACT OF SUBSCRIPTION TO CABLE TV ON HOUSEHOLD BEHAVIOR

BEHAVIOR	PERCENT INCREASE	PERCENT DECREASE
Eating out	1.7%	7.0%
Movies out	1.8	47.4
Attending sports events	2.1	9.2
Driving miles/week	1.4	11.8
Home entertaining	17.4	2.5
Family together time/ week	14.4	4.1
Late night TV viewing	50.4	1.9
Radio listening time/ week	3.3	15.2
Reading time/week	2.9	19.3
Hobby time/week	2.4	14.5

SOURCE: *Journal of Advertising Research*, August/September 1983. Order of chart listings revised by author, with permission.

[2]A Nielsen term referring to counties in the top 25 SMSAs plus all other counties that either have populations of over 150,000 or are within metropolitan areas of over 150,000 population.

There are in fact two different television universes now: the regular television universe and the cable universe, which the Cabletelevision Advertising Bureau (CAB) has termed "Cable America: Too Big and Too Important to Ignore."

From an advertiser's standpoint, this should suggest two things. One is that cable households are less likely to be reached by other media (print, radio, outdoor); the other is that since it is cable which is causing these changes, advertisers must use cable to reach these lost households. Already hundreds of national and local advertisers have availed themselves of the many advantages of cable. Advertising expenditures in cable have grown from a few hundred thousand dollars in the late 1970s to over $500 million in 1984, and they are expected to grow more than tenfold to $5.7 billion by 1994.

CABLE ADVERTISING REVENUE GROWTH ESTIMATES
(Millions of Dollars)

YEAR	CABLE NETWORK	NATIONAL/LOCAL SPOT	TOTAL
1980	$ 50.0	$ 8.0	$ 58.0
1981	104.9	16.7	121.7
1982	195.0	31.8	226.8
1983	303.0	50.4	353.4
1984	434.0	80.0	514.0
1985	597.0	128.0	725.0
1986	790.0	205.0	995.0
1987	1,045.0	308.0	1.353.0
1988	1,347.0	431.0	1,778.0
1989	1,678.0	560.0	2,238.0
1990	2,093.0	672.0	2,765.0
1991	2,543.0	806.0	3,349.0
1992	3,078.0	967.0	4,045.0
1993	3,712.0	1,160.0	4,872.0
1994	4,380.0	1,334.0	5,714.0

SOURCE: *Cable TV Advertising* (newsletter), March 22, 1984. © 1984 Paul Kagan Associates, Inc.

Many claims have been made for and about cable, not all of them realistic. Cable is not a miracle worker, nor a panacea. It will not create markets for unsalable products. It is, however, a powerful medium that can be a valuable tool for advertisers who use it properly. This book is designed to introduce you to cable and to help you learn how to use it to your best advantage.

TWO

REASONS TO USE CABLE

In deciding which media to use, an advertiser must evaluate each available medium by the advantages it offers in relation to marketing goals. Cable's technology and programming give it not only a combination of the best that other media have to offer—the sight/sound/motion impact of television, and the low cost and selectivity of radio—but also a number of unique benefits and opportunities for advertisers that may not be quite as obvious.

THE CABLE AUDIENCE

• *Targeting of specific audiences.*   Traditional television has been built on the philosophy of presenting programming with the broadest possible appeal for the time period it is being broadcast. Critics have referred to this as the "lowest common denominator" or "least objectionable programming" approach. Advertisers, therefore, have little opportunity to use television selectively; they cannot deliver messages to target audiences without substantial waste. Cable has highly specialized programming targeted to specific audiences, which enables advertisers to reach viewers who are really likely to be customers. There is less waste and a more efficient and effective advertising buy for each advertising dollar.

5

• *Upscale audiences, greater purchasing power.*   Since cable is a service that must be bought and paid for monthly, it is logical to assume that it is to be found largely in households that have discretionary buying power. Dozens of studies conducted over the past ten years by research companies, advertising agencies, and cable companies have consistently corroborated this, showing that the cable audience has the demographics most advertisers are looking for. Cable households have above-average incomes, are better-educated, have higher-level occupations, and primarily fall within the 18–49 age range.

CHARACTERISTICS	TOTAL U.S. %	TOTAL U.S. INDEX	CABLE HOUSEHOLDS (INDEX)	NONCABLE HOUSEHOLDS (INDEX)
Age.				
18–34	40.8	100	108	95
35–44	16.8	100	111	93
45–54	13.6	100	101	99
55 +	28.8	100	82	110
Income:				
$40,000 +	22.7	100	123	87
$30,000–$39,999	18.6	100	115	91
$20,000–$29,999	22.8	100	102	99
$10,000–$19,999	21.3	100	87	108
Under $10,000	14.6	100	60	123
Education:				
Graduated college	15.5	100	115	91
Attended college	16.9	100	113	92
Graduated HS	39.2	100	102	99
Did not graduate HS	28.4	100	82	111
Employment:				
Management/ Professional	14.3	100	117	90
Other employment	44.9	100	110	94
Not employed	40.8	100	83	110
HH Size:				
5 +	17.7	100	102	89
3–4	40.6	100	114	92
2	30.0	100	93	104
1	11.7	100	69	119

Base: Adults.
SOURCE: Mediamark Research Inc., Spring 1984.

Not only do cable households have high overall incomes, they also tend to have and use their greater disposable incomes; they buy more new cars, major appliances, and other high-ticket items than do noncable households. They also are more likely to be involved with the technology of television, owning VCRs, and other high-tech entertainment equipment.

	ADULTS IN CABLE HOUSEHOLDS (INDEX)	ADULTS IN NONCABLE HOUSEHOLDS (INDEX)
Purchased in Last 12 Months		
New car	124	86
Dishwasher	124	85
Microwave cookware	119	89
Lawn maintenance service	120	89
Hand tool outfit	128	84
4 to 8 videotapes/videodiscs	120	87
Home or personal computer	141	75
Computer/video games	129	83
Stereo receiver or amplifier	134	79
Headphones	127	85
Prerecorded cassette	123	86
35mm SLR camera	118	91
Diamond ring	116	90
Individual Retirement Account	120	88
Stocks	126	85
Own videocassette recorder	112	92
Shop at mall or large shopping center	116	91
Play golf	125	85
Play tennis	117	90
Own vacation or weekend home	123	87
Are frequent foreign air travelers	130	81

SOURCE: Mediamark Research Inc., Spring 1984.

• *Households that watch more television overall but less regular network television.*   As the following chart indicates, in 1983 cable households watched 53 hours a week, as contrasted with 46 hours a week for noncable households, yet the broadcast networks' share of viewing was significantly smaller—NBC dropped from 24 to 18 (a 25 percent loss), ABC from 26 to 19 (a 27 percent loss), and CBS from 29 to 21 (a 28 percent loss)—while independent television stations dropped from a 20 to a 14 share (a 30 percent loss). (The figures on which this chart is based may be found on the table on page 31.)

DISTRIBUTION OF VIEWING
Monday-Sunday, 24 Hours

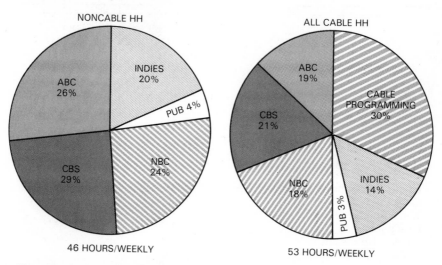

NONCABLE HH

INDIES
20%

ABC
26%

PUB 4%

CBS
29%

NBC
24%

46 HOURS/WEEKLY

ALL CABLE HH

ABC
19%

CABLE
PROGRAMMING
30%

CBS
21%

NBC
18%

INDIES
14%

PUB 3%

53 HOURS/WEEKLY

Note: Totals exceed 100% due to multiset usage.
SOURCE: A.C. Nielsen Monthly Cable TV Status Reports (NTI), January–December 1983. New-style reports used.

Over the next six months, not only did viewing in cable households continue to increase more than in noncable households, so did the decline in network shares. Viewing shares for NBC, ABC and CBS were 29 percent, 27 percent, and 31 percent lower, respectively, in cable households, while independents lost share points in both categories. (See chart on page 9.)

FLEXIBILITY AND LOWER COSTS

• *Zeroing in on geographic areas within markets.*   Radio and television are broadcast media, and as that name indicates, cover wide geographic areas without clearly definable borders. For advertisers looking to reach specific areas or locations, broadcast

DISTRIBUTION OF VIEWING
Monday-Sunday, 24 Hours

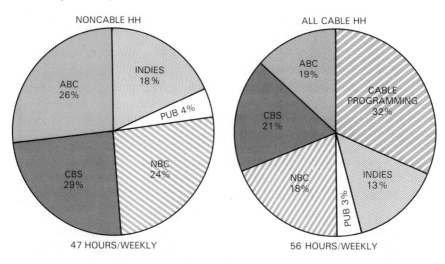

NONCABLE HH

ABC 26%
INDIES 18%
PUB 4%
CBS 29%
NBC 24%

47 HOURS/WEEKLY

ALL CABLE HH

ABC 19%
CABLE PROGRAMMING 32%
CBS 21%
NBC 18%
PUB 3%
INDIES 13%

56 HOURS/WEEKLY

Note: Totals exceed 100% due to multiset usage.
SOURCE: A.C. Nielsen Monthly Cable TV Status Reports (NTI), January–July 1984. New-style reports used.

television can be a very wasteful buy, as they have to pay not only for the audience in their target area(s), but also for viewers outside the area who receive the signal. This is less true for low-power broadcast stations, which have smaller coverage areas but also relatively limited influence in their markets. Cable systems are franchised and operated on an individual community basis, making it possible to fine-tune coverage down to a zip code or even house-by-house selectivity.

  • *Low-cost advertising.*   Cable's lower advertising rates make it possible for smaller advertisers to take advantage of the sight-and-sound impact of television that they could not afford on broadcast television. Cable also lets all advertisers' media dollars go further by giving advertisers the chance to make more efficient and less costly buys.

  • *Sponsorship opportunities.*   Given cable's low cost, it is now possible for both national and local advertisers to sponsor entire programs, series, or events on cable at a reasonable cost.

Some advertisers are having original programs made for them (see Chapter 8).

• *Flexibility of commercial length.*   Many cable networks and systems can provide advertisers with commercial breaks that can vary in length to meet clients' needs. The standard broadcast television commercial length is 30 seconds; with cable, you can use spots ranging from 10 to 120 seconds or even more. A whole new type of commercial, the *infomercial,* where advertisers take up to ten minutes to present their products in a relaxed, informative manner, has been made possible through cable (see Chapter 7).

• *Opportunity to build frequency of exposure.*   It is not often that you can have a successful advertising effort by showing a commercial once. To make an impact in terms of numbers of people reached and overall impression made, a commercial must be run several times. With cable's lower time costs, an advertiser can buy several spots for the same amount of money that a comparably placed television spot would cost, and those spots can be more effectively targeted, adding to the overall efficiency of the buy.

• *A multimedia medium.*   Cable systems' service to their subscribers goes beyond the actual cable programming, and you can make use of this to extend the reach and impact of your cable buy. Program guides, bill stuffers, and other media can all be adapted to coordinate with and supplement video advertising (see Chapter 9).

• *Commercials that fit programming environments.*   A single commercial is rarely right for all audiences, yet so often television advertising campaigns are limited by financial and/or creative restrictions to just that. With cable, an advertiser can afford to create and use a variety of different commercials and creative approaches, each designed specifically for the audience being reached during a particular program or set of programs.

• *Low-cost testing of new products and advertising.*   The low cost of producing and running cable advertising makes experimenting with new commercials or testing new products much more economical than with broadcast television. As one advertiser put it, if it turns out you have a turkey on your hands, you won't have spent a fortune to find that out.

• ***Merchandisability.***   In using cable, you can motivate your sales force and position yourself to your customers as being in the forefront of the new electronic media. Adding cable to your advertising media mix gives your salespeople a reason to make additional sales calls on trade accounts to let them know what you are doing.

THREE

PLANNING CONSIDERATIONS FOR CABLE ADVERTISING

It is not enough to say, "OK, sounds good to me; I think I'll use cable to do my advertising." Whether you are dealing with a multimillion-dollar budget for a nationally distributed product or debating whether you can afford a couple of hundred dollars to advertise a small retail business, the key word is planning. I cannot overemphasize that cable should be looked at *in the context of an overall media plan,* and the decision to be made is whether cable can help you achieve your objectives as part of that plan.

It will be much easier to make that decision once you are not only familiar, but comfortable with cable. Although it is not necessary that you understand the mechanics of how cable signals are delivered to the home,[1] you should at least be aware of what is out there in the way of programming. If you have cable yourself, spend a week or two taking a good look at the various network and local offerings on your system. Obtain and read several different program guides to see what kind of formats are used. If you do not personally have access to cable programming, or if you have additional questions, arrange to visit a nearby system and talk with an advertising representative or the system manager. For news of

[1]For those who are interested, Appendix A contains an explanation of how cable signals are distributed and received.

and perspective on cable advertising and the cable industry as a whole, a variety of trade periodicals are available, some of which are listed in Appendix C.

For best results, cable should be included in your media planning as a matter of course, not as something extra to be looked at if there's any money left after the other media have been given their allocations. Major advertising agencies such as BBDO already follow this practice.

SETTING YOUR OBJECTIVES

Because cable offers new ways of targeting prospective customers, businesses interested in taking advantage of these opportunities often find it necessary to stop and think about just who they want to target and to what end—considerations that might not have been addressed in earlier advertising plans designed simply to reach as many bodies as possible within a given area.

All advertisers have special concerns that they face in planning their advertising. Retailers, for example, have to deal with factors not faced by packaged goods manufacturers, such as store locations, competitors within their trading area(s), pricing changes, available co-op funds, shifting customer profiles, seasonal sales trends, and general economic conditions peculiar to the trading area. They also often have less lead time for planning and must be flexible enough to deal with regularly changing market conditions and opportunities.

Many businesses have operating and advertising plans extending as far as five to ten years in the future, but day-to-day pressures for others often make it easy for managers to overlook important market analysis and longer-range planning. You may find it helpful to take some time to think through the answers to the following questions, which deal with the current and future status of your business. The answers will help you put your overall business in focus, which can be particularly valuable in building an advertising approach.

• *Your business and your competition.*   In a now-classic article in the *Harvard Business Review*, "Marketing Myopia," Theodore Levitt pointed out the need for businesses to determine exactly what business they are in. The decline of the railroads, he suggested, was largely a result of their not being able to adapt themselves to new trends. They considered themselves as solely in the *railroad* business, rather than in the *transportation* business. Similarly, the motion picture studios found themselves in trouble when they were unable to deal realistically with the advent of television. Again, they considered themselves to be in the *movie* business, rather than the *entertainment* business (though it is interesting to note that most of the surviving studios are now active in television, cable, home video, and video games as well as in films).

Changing market conditions make it essential that you set realistic objectives. It is also important that you understand your competitive position in the marketplace and have a clear idea of what has to be done to improve your position. These factors are vital for advertising planning, since basic copy and creative themes must reflect your overall business objectives.

How would you describe your business?

Who are your major competitors?

What are your competitive advantages?

What are your competitive disadvantages?

What competitive improvements are you planning or would like to see, both short- and long-term?

• *Your customers.*   Every business thinks it has a fix on its prime customers, though few actually take time to quantify that impression on a regular basis. When it comes to advertising, this is one of the most important considerations to be addressed, because it can substantially affect the effectiveness of the media buy. It has been said that cable lets the advertiser use a rifle rather than a shotgun to reach prospective customers—however, you do have to know where to aim. Knowing the demographics of your desired customers will make it much easier to choose from cable's selective programming in making your media buys, as well as enabling you to make specially targeted creative and promotional efforts.

Who are your prime customers?

Men (%)?

Women (%)?

Teens (%)?

Children (%)?

Age?
Income?
Marital status?
Geographic areas drawn from?
What shifts or improvements in type of customer would be desirable?

• *Sales and promotions.*   Traditionally, businesses, especially retailers, have repeated a select group of promotions, often beyond their wearout stage, to the point that many have taken on historic lives of their own. In today's competitive world, it is important to keep reviewing not only the effectiveness and productivity of your own promotions, but also to keep track of what your competitors are doing.

Most stores have a certain "rhythm" of activity, as measured by peak sales months or days. The most effective retail advertising matches those store rhythms, and since as a rule even the most expensive or powerful advertising cannot change them, it is best to "go with the flow." Careful periodic surveys of your own business's rhythm will help ensure that the timing and content of your advertising and promotions are in sync with it.

What are your key selling periods?
What are your peak sales months?
What are your peak sales days?
In order of importance, list your most important annual sales events (include dates).
What is the best promotion you have ever run?
Why did it work as well as it did?

• *Co-op advertising for retailers.*   Countless millions of co-op dollars go unused each year. This is partly due to the fact that many retailers do not have adequate systems for tracking available funds. Advertisers who want to get the most out of their available co-op dollars are now working with their local cable systems to take advantage of the co-op allowances being authorized for cable. The two key questions for retailers are these:

What brand names do you carry?
What are your sources of co-op funds?

Manufacturers who are considering cable advertising should also be sure that cable is included as an eligible medium in any of their co-op plans as one way to expand local advertising coverage. (For those readers not already familiar with or using co-op, that subject will be covered in detail in Chapter 11.)

• *Your advertising.*   Since advertising plays such a substantial business-building role, it should be reviewed constantly for effectiveness and efficiency. The following questions are designed to help you make such an evaluation. While most call for objective answers, in some cases there will obviously be some measure of subjectivity involved. You may be more familiar with some media than with others because of past experience with them; it is important, though, that you remain open-minded as far as all media are concerned, due to changes both in market conditions and in consumer media usage patterns.

How is your current advertising budget broken down, in terms of both actual dollars and percentage of total budget?
Newspapers?
Television?
Cable?
Radio?
Magazines?
Direct mail?
Outdoor?
Other?

Has your advertising budget increased enough to cover rises in media costs? If not, do you feel the overall impact of your advertising budget has declined?

How do you evaluate the strengths and weaknesses of each medium?
Newspapers?
Television?
Cable?
Radio?
Magazines?
Direct mail?
Outdoor?
Other?

What do you like to emphasize in your advertising approach (image, price, location, selection, service)?

What would you like to have your advertising investment produce in terms of results?

Are you currently seeing those results? If not, why not?

If the answer to the last question is "no," then it is definitely time to think about how cable can help you change that answer.

A WORD TO AGENCIES

Although a number of advertising agencies have taken significant initiatives to explore cable's opportunities and bring their clients into cable, I frequently hear comments from both advertisers and agency personnel that their own agency has not been moving into cable as quickly as they would like it to. Often it seems that this is because the agency people are not aware or convinced of cable's benefits or are not sure how to use it. I hope that this book will help alleviate such problems where they may exist, but I would also like to cite three suggestions offered by McKinsey & Company, Inc., as part of its conclusion to a year-long analysis of agency practices and attitudes about cable as ways to bring cable efficiently into the working mainstream:

• *Get top management interested in cable.*   Agency top management must provide the initiative. Since policy decisions will be of strategic significance to both you and your clients, they should not fall by default to the client or to the middle or junior management levels within the agency.

• *Develop buying criteria and scan your client list.*   Here again, agency top management must take the lead. Once you have established criteria for evaluating cable, no cable opportunity that represents a real marketing value should be allowed to slip by.

• *Create a focal point for cable in the organization.*   One possible way to do this is to set up a task force that includes representatives from all functional areas within the agency and acts as a clearinghouse for cable. By gathering a group of people who are or will become experts in cable and how it relates to their respective areas, ideas can be promptly and thoroughly evaluated and recommendations made to senior account representatives and clients. The task force should be led by a senior executive whose primary responsibility is cable, and who will serve as final arbiter for the task force and as the client advocate.

To these I would add one more recommendation: that top management provide adequate training and support for the rest of the agency. In a number of cases, I have found that an agency's top executives are very enthusiastic about cable, but the rest of the staff (especially the media buyers) are only minimally familiar with it.

MAKING THE CABLE BUY

A few words about actually buying cable advertising are appropriate here. I do not intend to go into detail on the mechanics of media planning, on which a number of excellent books have already been written, but I want to address some of the most frequently raised questions relating to the topic.

Contrary to popular opinion, buying cable really is not difficult or mysterious. Cable ad salespeople are prepared and eager to work with you to develop effective and efficient advertising buys. They can use their knowledge of programming and subscriber counts and characteristics to help you find new ways of making use of the new creativity and flexibility to be found in cable. Many are also veterans of broadcast sales and/or the advertising business, so they speak your language and understand your concerns.

Basically there are three ways of buying cable: nationally, on cable networks or through national spot buys; locally, on individual cable systems; and regionally, on groups of systems by way of interconnects and rep firms. Each of these will be explored in the chapters that follow.

Some people say they can't deal with the sheer number of cable outlets, and don't know how to find them. Actually, there are about two dozen advertiser-supported national cable networks, which are listed in Appendix B. While there are over 8,000 cable systems in operation around the country, only about 1,000 of them are currently equipped to accept local advertising (although these systems serve more than one-third of all cable subscribers). These numbers may be larger than those for the commercial television outlets (three major networks and about 800 local stations), but they are much smaller than the number of national and local newspapers and magazines available to advertisers. The problem comes for advertisers looking to make local or regional spot buys outside their immediate market, where they can find the local system(s) in the phone book, because there are really no publications for cable comparable to the Standard Rate and Data Service (SRDS) spot TV and radio rate directories. The National Cable Television Association (NCTA) published three annual editions (1980–82) of its *Cable Advertising Directory* based on surveys of its member systems. Although each edition was a marked improvement over its predecessor, they all tended to suffer from outdated and incomplete listings. In 1981 the TAG Cable Information Company introduced its *TAG Cable Advertising Directory,* a quarterly looseleaf service that provided information on over 800 systems and was known for its accuracy and detail. Unfortunately, publication of the TAG directory was suspended in March 1984 when the company underwent a major reorganization.

CAB publishes a directory which lists interconnects and rep firms and the systems and markets they serve, and the A.C. Nielsen Company operates a service called Cable On-Line Data Exchange, utilizing a computerized data base covering over 8,000 cable systems from which information on up to 250 characteristics of each system can be obtained on request. Either of these should make things a little easier for buyers.

Most of the other popular questions concern issues regarding audience measurement and research for cable, which are discussed in Chapter 4.

FOUR

RESEARCH IN CABLE

When faced with cable for the first time, most advertisers and agencies that are used to making traditional television buys will immediately call for ratings, shares, and other numbers, often at a level of precision greater than that which they require from other media, to justify any consideration of cable. The cable industry is very sensitive to the legitimate need and demand for audience measurement, and considerable progress has been made in this area.

Although advertiser-supported cable is only a few years old, a substantial amount of information is now available about the impact cable is having on television audience distribution. In September 1983, Gregory Blaine of Foote, Cone & Belding told an Advertising Research Foundation conference that while media decision makers may not have all the research they may *want*, they certainly have all the research they *need* to make good cable buying decisions. Most decision makers, he added, seem to have overlooked the fundamental premise that the degree of precision used in measuring information must match the degree of risk involved in the decision. Given that, he concluded that then-current cable audience measurement was suitable for advertisers to make plans to spend 7 to 10 percent of their national broadcast budgets on cable. The situation has improved since then.

The A.C. Nielsen Company tracks cable network viewing on a regular basis (most of the major networks are now on its meters), and also provides a variety of special studies on both network and system viewership. The Arbitron Ratings Company conducts tests of local viewing levels on individual systems. Simmons Market Research Bureau and Mediamark Research Inc. (MRI) are two of the companies active in demographic and media/product usage research in the cable universe. Broadcast Advertisers Reports (BAR) monitors commercial activity on four major cable networks. Dozens of other companies, including Opinion Research Corporation, The ELRA Group, Information & Analysis, The NPD Group, and Marquest Media Services, among others, also do customized reports on cable-related information.

In reviewing any numbers offered by cable networks, ratings services, or other sources, advertisers must clearly understand that such traditional measurement techniques as diaries and telephone recall seriously underreport cable viewership, and that the actual audience ratings for cable are probably twice as large as those reported using these methodologies.

There are several reasons why this happens. One major reason is that in many cases the average viewer is not really familiar with all the cable programming services he or she watches. While the viewer may identify standard broadcast channels by their FCC-assigned channel numbers and/or call letters, if in a telephone interview he says he is watching "the movie channel," you cannot be sure whether he means in fact The Movie Channel or another pay cable movie service such as Home Box Office or Showtime. Likewise, "the sports channel" could be ESPN, USA Cable Network, or any one of a number of regional sports networks, such as Sportschannel or Madison Square Garden Cablevision. The problem becomes even more complicated when systems market services under names other than their given ones, and/or when those names are identical or similar to those of other services, such as a system offering an HBO/Cinemax package as "Show Time!".

Identification by channel numbers, too, is virtually useless, since cable services do not have assigned channel numbers, nor are they positioned on cable systems' converters in any kind of uniform manner; the positioning of broadcast stations on converters also may not match their licensed channels. On the converters in my home, for example, the VHF television station positions match their channel numbers, but this is not so for the UHF stations. Were a ratings service to ask me what I was watching and I to reply "channel 31," that could mean I was watching either USA Cable Network (which is on channel 31 on our converter) or WNYC-TV (the New York City public television station which is on channel 31 of the broadcast band but channel 12 on our converter).

Complicating the matter even further is the fact that several different types of equipment can be used to receive and translate cable signals, each of which may use a different identification system and all of which may be used in the same cable systems. For example, the same channel might be identified on older (pre-LED) converters as channel Q, on newer converters with numeric readouts as channel 25, and on a particular brand of cable-ready television set as channel 94—but all refer to Cable News Network on that system.

In 1980 a group of advertising agency research executives and cable executives formed the Ad Hoc Cable Measurement Committee. The goal of the committee was to determine alternative ways of accurately measuring television viewing in homes that subscribe to cable television. After intensive discussions of the problems in using traditional audience measurement techniques, it was decided that a new approach was called for. The committee contacted 68 research companies and asked them for proposals on how they would attempt to address the problem. From this review, the A.C. Nielsen Company was selected to work with the committee in designing a methodology study.

In 1981 the CAB/NCTA Research Standards Committee was established, succeeding the Ad Hoc Committee. The Standards Committee was comprised of 15 leading research executives from cable networks, MSOs, advertising sales representatives, and trade associations. They took the recommendations of the Ad Hoc Committee, refined them, and developed the seven techniques that would be tested in the Cable Audience Methodology Study (CAMS). Those seven techniques included four diary and three telephone techniques:

The standard Nielsen NSI diary

A personal rostered daypart diary

A household rostered daypart diary

A personal rostered half-hour diary

Seven-day one-call-per-day telephone recall
One-day-only aided telephone recall
One-day-only unaided telephone recall

The rostered diaries were specially developed by Nielsen for CAMS.

CAMS was fielded by Nielsen in June 1982. The two systems selected for the test were the Gillcable system in San Jose, California, and the Warner Amex Cable system in Columbus, Ohio. Both systems offered a wide variety of programming types, including advertiser-supported cable networks, superstations, distant stations, local origination, pay cable networks, pay-per-view and must-carries. This was important because it is in this type of programming environment that traditional measurement techniques have fallen short. The validator for the study was a telephone coincidental test consisting of 60,000 calls to cable viewers on the two systems and, between 11 P.M. and 9 A.M., when telephone coincidentals could not be conducted, passive monitoring of viewing activity in Columbus by way of the Warner Amex system's interactive QUBE feature.

The preliminary CAMS findings were made public in February 1983. It must be understood that the purpose of the test was not to get specific audience measurements on the two systems selected, but to test the reliability of each of the methodologies. Nevertheless, in summarizing the study, Nielsen claimed that "[c]able channels were . . . almost always being understated." For example, the telephone coincidental techniques revealed that the average household rating (percentage of total television households) for basic cable, Monday–Friday 9 A.M.–11 P.M., was 5.4. The standard television diary, however, estimated the same rating as 3.4, a net undercounting of *37 percent.* Similarly, a coincidental rating for persons 12+ viewing basic cable of 3.1 versus a diary rating of 1.4 represented an undercount of *55 percent* of the viewing audience. The CAMS findings were independently corroborated by Arbitron's Two-Way Cable/Cable Diary Test conducted in June 1982, which tested four methodologies in four cable systems.

Nielsen and Arbitron have continued to pursue those methodologies which have shown the most promise in testing to the point that they can be widely recognized as reliable. Assisting them in their efforts is the Cable Research Advisory Council, the CAB-founded entity that has succeeded the Standards Committee.

Until such measurement techniques can be developed and put into regular use, it may help to think of cable coverage in the same way people have been buying print advertising for decades— namely, by circulation. After all, all a newspaper or magazine can tell you for certain is how many copies have been sold. Beyond that, readership estimates are about as valid as television ratings.

In the meantime, there are other ways to discover the impact of cable advertising. Obviously, direct-response advertising can be tracked by the resulting orders; "direct-response without the 800 number," as Times Mirror Cable Television regional sales manager Charles Jones called it, can be achieved with promotional commercials offering discounts or giveaways, or with commercials for products or services not advertised elsewhere. On the local level, you are likely to find people volunteering that they saw your ad (see page 43). In practice, it seems one of the best ways to get that response is to make a mistake. In Harrisburg, Pennsylvania, a skeptical sales manager at an auto dealership that had been running cable advertising for two months became a believer when the cable system accidentally tagged an incorrect financing rate to one of his commercials and in the next two days a dozen people came in to ask him about the erroneous rate. During a spot break in one of the cable programs I made in Ithaca, New York, an engineer at the cable system ran the wrong tape of a commercial for a pharmacy (an outtake with the announcer swearing as he fumbled his lines halfway through); the store owner didn't cancel his advertising contract after that only because so many people came into the store the next day to comment on the commercial.

There are, of course, more sophisticated ways to measure advertising effectiveness than by the fallout from embarrassing errors in commercials. In 1983–84, Management Science Associates produced a computerized report developed by CAB called B.A.S.I.C. (Broadcast Advertising Schedules Impacted by Cable) that assessed the difference in advertising weight between cable and noncable households for all brands appearing on the three broadcast television networks. The B.A.S.I.C. reports were produced by combining BAR records of network advertising schedules with Nielsen Television Index (NTI) audience estimates. Over 1,000 schedules were processed for each of eight monthly reporting periods corresponding to the Nielsen Audience Demographic cycle. Overall corporate delivery and brand schedules were analyzed, with up to 18 demographic breakouts provided for the total television, all cable, pay cable, and noncable universes.

Special tabulations that have been done on advertising schedules which include over-the-air television and cable show that both reach and frequency increase substantially in cable households when advertiser-supported cable is added to the media mix. The first such tabulation of this type, a special NTI report called *New Dimensions of Television*, concluded that cable adds substantially to the reach of network television advertising in both pay cable and basic cable households, with the reach and gross rating points added by cable tending to be greatest in households with incomes of over $20,000.

Even as research improves in cable, it is important to remember that cable is as much a qualitative buy as a quantitative one. CPMs (cost per thousand) and GRPs (gross rating points) are not adequate to evaluate cable buys. Several media experts have offered alternatives to these measurements, such as CPB (cost per buyer) and CPP (in this case, cost per purchase), that focus on the value of advertising given the actual results generated rather than the number of warm bodies reached by a commercial.

As Burt Manning, chairman and CEO of J. Walter Thompson U.S.A., has put it: ". . . operating on numbers alone can stop the brain from functioning. . . . [S]ometimes they can inhibit media judgment and stifle the daring, the unusual, the creative media idea that can leverage the media dollar in cable as in no other medium." Don't let the traditional numbers game stand in the way of your taking advantage of the opportunities cable offers.

FIVE

NATIONAL CABLE ADVERTISING

Television has been by far the leading national advertising medium since reaching its maturity in the mid-1950s. The dominance of the three major networks—ABC, CBS, and NBC—and their affiliates has enabled advertisers to quickly and efficiently reach a large share of all households in the United States. During prime time, for example, the three networks traditionally have had a combined share of over 90 percent of viewing in television households, with the balance going to independent and public television stations.

The ratings trends of the 1980s show that the broadcast network affiliates are losing their monopoly as providers of television programming. They are losing to independent broadcast stations, pay cable, basic cable, video games, videotapes and discs, and other forms of home entertainment. Changes in viewing patterns in cable households are primarily responsible for the overall decline in the total ratings and shares reported for network television programming. In the early stages of cable's development, the importance of these changes was not as evident because data about cable households were averaged in with those for noncable households, effectively providing a "statistical cushion" for the networks to lean on. As cable penetration increased and studies

BROADCAST NETWORK AFFILIATE SHARES BY DAYPART

☐ Cable HH   ▨ Non-Cable HH

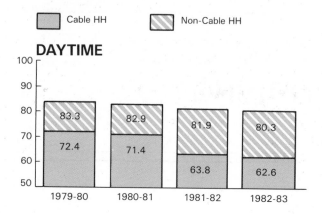

DAYTIME

	1979-80	1980-81	1981-82	1982-83
Non-Cable	83.3	82.9	81.9	80.3
Cable	72.4	71.4	63.8	62.6

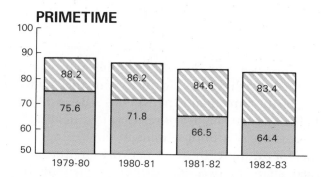

PRIMETIME

	1979-80	1980-81	1981-82	1982-83
Non-Cable	88.2	86.2	84.6	83.4
Cable	75.6	71.8	66.5	64.4

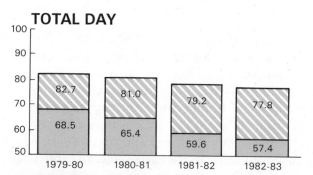

TOTAL DAY

	1979-80	1980-81	1981-82	1982-83
Non-Cable	82.7	81.0	79.2	77.8
Cable	68.5	65.4	59.6	57.4

For the total day broadcast affiliate shares are declining almost 3 times more quickly in cable than non-cable households.

SOURCE: A.C. Nielsen Monthly Cable TV Status Reports (NTI). Average of November, February, May and July reports. Old style used throughout.

began to separate the two types of household data, the differences became clear. The chart on p. 28 shows how, over a four-year period, viewing of network affiliates declined three times more rapidly in cable households, because they had a choice of alternative programming, than in households without cable.

All indications are that this trend will continue, with prime time broadcast network affiliates' shares declining to as low as 59 percent by 1990 by some estimates, a level that has already been reached on a total day basis. At the same time, viewing of advertiser-supported cable networks has steadily increased.

With many critics suggesting that cable viewership is mostly going to the pay services, it is worth noting that in the table on p. 30 of 1983 viewership, the numbers for basic cable and nonnetwork broadcast are in fact the same as those for all cable households, with the increased pay cable viewing coming at the expense of the broadcast network affiliates.

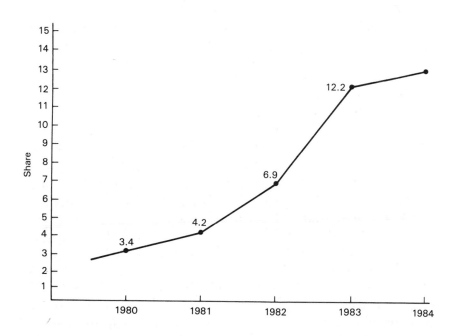

SOURCE: A.C. Nielsen Monthly Cable TV Status Reports (NTI). Average of reports for each year.

HOUSEHOLD AUDIENCE SHARES
MONDAY-SUNDAY, 24 HOURS

	ALL TV HH	NONCABLE HH	CABLE HH	PAY CABLE HH
Broadcast Affiliates:				
ABC	23%	26%	19%	18%
CBS	25	29	21	18
NBC	21	24	18	17
Total	71	80	59	54
Other Broadcast:				
Independent	17	20	14	14
Public	3	4	3	3
Total	20	24	17	17
Advertiser-Supported Cable:				
Cable-originated	5	—	11	11
Superstations	4	—	8	8
Total	9	—	19	19
Pay Cable	5	—	11	18
Total Cable Services	14	—	30	36

Note: Totals exceed 100% due to multiset usage.
SOURCE: A.C. Nielsen Monthly Cable TV Status Reports (NTI), January–December 1983. New-style reports used.

The NPD/Electronic Media Tracking Service has found that during a typical day, 63 percent of all cable households tune in to some advertiser-supported cable service; 88 percent tune in in the course of a week, and 95 percent in the course of a month.

The result of this ratings gap between the cable and noncable universes is that broadcast network programming is consistently underdelivering audiences in upscale cable households and, reciprocally, overdelivering them in noncable households.

The loss of program rating points in cable households translates directly into a loss of advertising effectiveness for broadcast advertising schedules. B.A.S.I.C. reports for May 1983 showed that of the 346 network television advertisers running commercials that month, *96 percent* underdelivered gross rating points (GRPs) in cable households, with over half of those underdelivering by 10 percent or more.

In order to reach the growing number of cable households being underdelivered by traditional television, advertisers have turned to cable networks as the only alternative video medium that can deliver a national audience.

AVERAGE BROADCAST NETWORK PROGRAM RATINGS AND RELATIVE AUDIENCE DELIVERY FOR SELECTED DEMOGRAPHICS

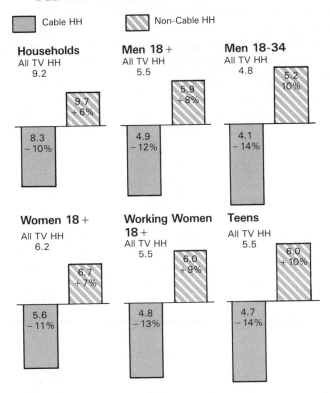

SOURCE: Broadcast Advertising Schedules Impacted by Cable derived from Broadcast Advertisers Reports, and A.C. Nielsen National Audience Demographics Reports, May 1983.

Many people seem to become confused when I talk about cable networks and affiliate cable systems, particularly in terms of how the two relate. It may help to remember that cable networks operate much like the broadcast television networks. All these networks provide programming that is distributed to viewers through local affiliates; for NBC, those affiliates have names like WXYZ and KTVO, while for CNN they have names like Cox Cable San Diego and Broward Cablevision. When you make a network buy, you are buying time within the network programming block, and your ad will be seen wherever the network signal is carried. The major difference is that while a television station will be an affiliate of only one of the three television networks, a cable system can be an affiliate of as many different cable networks as it chooses (and has channel capacity) to carry.

Like the commercial networks, cable networks offer anywhere from 1 to 12 minutes an hour to advertisers. They also leave time, usually 1 to 4 minutes an hour, open for local affiliates to sell (more about this in Chapter 6).

Unlike the broadcast networks, which have to try to be all things to all people, cable networks tend to devote all (or major segments) of their programming efforts to specific types of programming targeted to specific interests, much the way specialized magazines do. As a result, advertisers have a perfect opportunity to target the specific demographics they wish to reach. Commenting on the variety of different programming available on cable networks, Peter Spengler of Bristol-Myers has suggested that by 1987 we will all look back and wonder how three television networks could have served the needs of 200 million people. (Even now, many of us who have cable in our homes tend to suffer withdrawal symptoms when faced with television sets not so equipped).

Here are just a few examples of the types of programming being offered on an ongoing basis by cable networks, with some of the networks on which you'll find them.

• *News.*   Up-to-date national and international news coverage both in headline format and in more detailed presentations; sports news; weather reports; interviews with newsmakers; financial reports and discussions; some lifestyle and entertainment reports. *Cable News Network, CNN Headline News, The Weather Channel.*

• *Sports.*   Live and tape-delayed professional and college sports events; sports news reports; panel shows with sports figures; historical sports features. *ESPN, USA Cable Network, WTBS, plus a variety of regional sports networks, both basic and pay.*

• *Music.*   Music videos; live and taped concerts; music industry news; interviews with musicians. *MTV: Music Television, Country Music Television, The Nashville Network, USA Cable Network.*

• *Ethnic and international.*   A wide variety of English- and foreign-language programming aimed at specific ethnic and/or national audiences, including black, Spanish, Jewish, Oriental, French, etc. *Black Entertainment Television, SIN Television Network, National Jewish Television, Satellite Program Network.*

• *Cultural.*   Classical music concerts; opera; ballet; museum tours; literary discussions; profiles of great artists; classic and contemporary theater. *Arts & Entertainment Network.*

• *Children.*   Educational and entertainment programming specifically selected for children of diverse age groups. *Nickelodeon, USA Cable Network.*

• *Self-improvement.*   Programs on food and nutrition, fashion, home and auto care, diet and exercise; medical news and advice; counseling for personal and family problems. *Lifetime, USA Cable Network, Satellite Program Network.*

• *Financial.*   Stock and commodity market reports; business news and analysis; interviews with business executives and analysts; investment education and advice. *Financial News Network, Business Times, Cable News Network.*

Also included in the category of networks are what have become generically known as *superstations.* These are standard television broadcast stations which, in addition to broadcasting over the air in their FCC-licensed markets, transmit their signals around the country by satellite.[1] The original and best-known of

---

[1] Some people include in this category *all* broadcast stations carried by cable systems outside their broadcast markets, including radio stations distributed by satellite (WFMT (Chicago) in particular) and television stations distributed by microwave.

these stations is Ted Turner's SuperStation WTBS in Atlanta, which coined the term. There are only three other superstations: WOR-TV (Secaucus, NJ), WGN-TV (Chicago), and WPIX-TV (New York), although they have not been positioning themselves as such to advertisers. The viability of superstations as potential national cable advertising outlets was underscored in a major way in 1981, when the Ted Bates agency issued a report to its clients recommending that they divert an average of 5 percent of their prime time network television advertising budgets to superstation buys as one way of trying to recapture the audience being lost by the broadcast networks.[2]

Many major advertisers got into cable early. By the end of 1981, 85 percent of the top 200 nationally advertised brands (except cigarettes), including all of the top 50 brands, could be found on cable. Anheuser-Busch has probably been the most active cable advertising pioneer. Since 1978, it has run extended schedules on several cable networks, with the greatest emphasis on sports offerings; it has also sponsored a number of sports competitions, together with cable network coverage thereof. At the 1982 CAB Cable Advertising Conference, Charles B. Fruit, VP-corporate media director of Anheuser-Busch, explained why his company got into cable as early and as actively as it did: "[The three broadcast] networks can only program a limited amount of sports . . . we felt that the hardcore sports fan wanted more and would search it out. . . . Cable TV offered us another way to reach this important segment of our target audience. Cable TV also allowed us program and team associations prohibitively costly on network television." Two years later, Mr. Fruit again addressed the conference and noted that the company's early investment in ESPN had been paying off handsomely. Anheuser-Busch has also used MTV and other nonsports programming extensively to reach the young adult segment of the cable audience, while many of its distributors around the country have successfully used local cable to supplement the company's national buys.

[2]In 1984, Ted Bates's Walter Reichel indicated that the agency was revising its recommendation to include only the advertiser-supported cable networks and WTBS, dropping the other superstations. At an IRTS seminar a few months earlier, Doyle Dane Bernbach's Jay James also had suggested that a 5 percent diversion from prime time network television budgets to cable would be advisable for advertisers.

In what is probably the ultimate advertiser extension of a media buy, Anheuser-Busch launched a regional cable sports network in April 1984 as a joint venture with Tele-Communications, Inc., and Multimedia. Called Sports Time Cable Network, it offers sports events on an exclusive basis to cable subscribers in 15 midwestern states, and Anheuser-Busch, naturally, is the sole beer advertiser thereon. Mr. Fruit calls the network an illustration of the company's "further belief in cable as a sound business as well as an important advertising medium."

Bristol-Myers has been involved in cable programming as well as maintaining an active spot schedule on several cable networks. The company made major news in 1981 with the announcement of a ten-year, $40 million sponsorship agreement for a series on USA Cable Network, and has sponsored several other shows and events. Procter & Gamble also has been involved with many cable programming development projects and, not surprisingly, has emerged as a leader in cable. Other major cable advertisers include General Foods, General Mills, Ford Motor Company, Time Inc., American Home Products, and Toyota.

In addition to these and other large advertisers, a growing number of smaller companies have turned to cable, attracted by the combination of lower cost and selective programming. These include some companies, such as John Henry Shirtmakers, who had not previously used television but have found cable an attractive and affordable buy.

In later chapters we will see some of the ways these advertisers have presented their messages on cable, including the use of specially created cable commercials and sponsored programming.

SIX

LOCAL CABLE ADVERTISING

During the first thirty years of cable, there was little reason for cable system operators to be concerned with advertising. There was no network and little local programming in which time could be sold, and operators saw their revenues coming from selling subscriber hookups, not advertising. As the opportunities arose for systems to offer local advertising availabilities in national cable network programming as well as in local origination cable programming, the cable industry became serious about developing local advertising as a business. The major MSOs have all created and staffed advertising departments on both the corporate and system level and have been adding the equipment and personnel needed to serve advertisers. In assuming the CAB chairmanship in 1983, Jack Clifford, chairman of Colony Communications, said: "At Colony, we believe that advertising will be an equal contributor to subscriber revenues on our bottom line. We hope that other forward-looking cable companies will . . . share that same good fortune." The result is that, in a growing number of individual markets, cable offers a range of valuable and, in many ways, unique opportunities.

For national advertisers interested in spot buys, cable provides the ultimate in geographic and demographic targeting

37

not previously available with television. These same advantages are also there for the local advertiser, and for many it makes television an affordable and practical option for the first time. This is due in part to the way local cable franchises are set up.

Broadcast television licenses are issued by the FCC for as much geography as can be covered with the amount of power the station is authorized to use on its frequency, so that most television stations actually operate within a 50- to 100-mile radius of the cities they are ostensibly licensed to (exclusive of any additional coverage resulting from microwave or satellite distribution). Cable franchises are granted by and for individual municipal units—cities, towns, villages. Large cities may be divided into smaller sections for the purpose of awarding cable franchises. As a result, it is quite common to find adjacent communities served by different cable systems, although one is also likely to find groups of communities that have awarded franchises to the same company and are served by a single system encompassing all those franchises.

One of the reasons for the favorable cost advantages of cable over regular television is that cable helps to eliminate the tremendous waste factor for local advertisers. Most localized businesses build their customer bases from a relatively limited area, generally within a ten-mile radius. This is especially true for retailers or service establishments where the customer is required to come to the place of business. Not only is local broadcast television still fairly expensive, but it also reaches thousands, sometimes millions of people outside the geographic area of interest. This situation is almost universal in suburban areas around major cities—coincidentally the areas where cable is having its greatest growth.

To offer an example, a clothing store in the suburban town of Midville realistically expects to draw most of its clientele from within Midville and its half-dozen neighboring towns in Average County. Even if the budget required for broadcast television were available, the only stations the store could advertise on would be those in nearby Bigapple, which beam their signals out over a 60-mile radius. A commercial run thereon would be seen by people in Bigapple, a dozen surrounding counties, and parts of two or three adjoining states; although most of these viewers would not be potential customers of the store, it would still be paying to reach all of them. For but a fraction of the cost of this one television spot, the store could place an ad on the cable systems serving Average County, where its real market is.

Local cable systems offer two basic types of spots. One is network insertion, the other is local origination. In the first, advertisers can buy time in the local availabilities the networks allow the systems to sell. Their commercials therefore can appear during breaks in programming in major national cable networks.[1] The second provides for insertion during local programming produced by the system, programming that is generally of community nature and interest. This has an added image value for advertisers as being concerned community participants, as well as the intrinsic advertising value.

It should be noted that even before the development of national cable networks, many people were predicting a bright future for cable as a major local advertising medium, based on its potential for truly local interest programming. While there has been major activity in developing cable in cities, it is still very much a suburban or exurban phenomenon. Most suburban areas are served by television stations in nearby cities, but rarely do these stations cover stories or events of local interest to these communities on a regular basis. As one major-market city television news anchorman once put it: "I've got only four camera crews, and if I have to send one of them to the suburbs for a story I've lost them for the whole day [whereas within the city a crew can cover several stories in a day]."

As a result, local cable programming is generating more and more attention. In dozens of areas across the country, local newscasts produced by cable systems regularly draw large audiences, sometimes larger than those of the newscasts on local television stations. High school and college sports events carried by cable systems also are tremendously popular, especially where there is active community support for the teams; a few cable systems have even gotten contracts to produce and carry telecasts of

---

[1]It must be clearly understood that these local availabilities apply only to certain advertiser-supported cable networks; the cable system may not insert commercials into other network signals. The system cannot, for example, cut into a pay cable service such as HBO to run local commercials, and it is illegal for it to interrupt *any* standard broadcast signals (such as preempting an ABC network or KABC-TV local spot), which is why there are no local cable spots available on any of the superstations (WTBS, WOR-TV, WGN-TV, WPIX-TV).

local professional sports, such as American Cable Television's arrangement with the Phoenix Suns (NBA basketball). In the area of public service programming, systems regularly cover public hearings, local elections, city council (or equivalent) meetings, and other civic activities; educational programs produced with or by local schools, hospitals, or businesses are also standard fare.

In many cases, cable provides the only source of specialized programming for a community. In New Bedford and Fall River, Massachusetts, for example, there is a large Portuguese population not regularly served by the local Providence, Rhode Island, television stations, so the Colony Communications cable system there provides an entire channel of Portuguese-language programming, including news, novelas, entertainment, and sports (on which, by the way, they have been successfully selling advertising since 1976). Similarly, most of the local programming done by the Colony cable system serving the northwest Miami, Florida, suburbs has been on its own Spanish-language channel, Miavision.[2]

Local cable advertising is rapidly expanding as systems acquire the technical and administrative capability to provide such service. If you are interested in advertising on cable in your community, the simplest way to find out if you can do so is to call your local system and ask if it accepts advertising. If, though, you plan to make spot buys outside your own area, you need to find out where and if you can do so (see page 20).

Let's take a look at some local cable advertising success stories. As with any advertising situation, a variety of factors ultimately determine the success of a campaign. But in all these stories, there is one thing in common: The advertisers involved carefully identified their marketing objectives, then tailored cable advertising campaigns to meet these objectives. By taking advantage of cable's geographic and demographic selectivity and adding the right commercial creative approach, they put together the elements always present in successful advertising.

In the Olympia, Washington, area, Black Hills Distributing Company, a local distributor for Olympia Brewing Company

---

[2]Colony discontinued Miavision on March 1, 1984, when it leased the channel space to Spanish Cable Network. SCN programs a 24-hour advertiser-supported, Spanish-language cable service called HIT-TV, which is carried on leased channels by most systems in South Florida.

(makers of Hamm's Beer and other brands), ran a cable-only advertising campaign for a new 16-ounce Hamm's can just being introduced in the area. A series of four 30-second commercials were produced just for this effort by the coordinating rep firm's production company at a cost of under $2,000. During the three months in which these spots ran in local ESPN availabilities on two area systems, sales of the "Hammer" (as the 16-ounce can came to be known) more than doubled, jumping from its precampaign rank as the no. 31 seller of the 42 brands/sizes distributed by Black Hills to the no. 17 position. It also enjoyed an 80 percent overall sales increase in on-premise tavern sales, with the greatest gains made in taverns with cable.

The Midvale, Ohio, branch of Fisher Big Wheel (a chain of discount department stores) was aware of cable as an advertising medium ten years before it finally decided to run a holiday giveaway promotion to build needed Christmas store traffic. Over 15,000 customers responded to the promotion, which ran on the Times Mirror New Philadelphia, Ohio, system. The store has since run several additional cable-only sales promotions, including one that resulted in the sale of 180 hamsters in one week, and attributes a 21 percent gain in sales to its cable advertising.

In Lafayette, Indiana, a sporting goods store called The Athlete's Foot ran commercials on local cable for a particular brand of tennis shoe and ended up having to reorder it to keep up with the demand.

U.S. Cablevision, the Colony system serving Beacon, New York, helped sell out a rock concert in Poughkeepsie (a city about 15 miles north of Beacon). A popular rock group, The Tubes, was scheduled to play at the 3,000-seat Mid-Hudson Civic Center. Radio spots were aired on the leading 50,000-watt FM rock station in Poughkeepsie starting about a week before the cable spots were to be run, and during that week only 25 to 50 tickets were sold each day. The first day the cable spots appeared in the local availabilities on MTV, ticket sales jumped to 150 a day, and the concert sold out. (Two interesting side notes: One, this was at a time when sellout concerts were rare even for major acts, and The Tubes, while gaining in popularity through their MTV video exposure, were not exactly a supergroup; two, for technical reasons the system had MTV on a pay tier, and only about 10,000 of their 40,000 subscribers were receiving it.)

In Newport Beach, California, a yacht dealer ran a commercial with nothing but pictures of yachts running in a harbor, tagged at the end with only the dealer's name and slogan (no address or phone). The first weekend the spot ran, four yachts were sold.

Class Printing of Fairfield, Connecticut, reported that the local cable advertising schedule it ran "created more recognition in our marketing area than anything we've used in our 12 years of business."

Total Tan, a tanning salon in McHenry, Illinois, had been promoting itself through flyers and newspapers. It ran a commercial on Lakes Cablevision eight times a day across CNN, ESPN, USA, and MTV in order to reach all demographic levels. Soon after the spots started running, business had increased over 200 percent.

McHenry Nautilus, a health spa, had been closed for remodeling. It decided to try to build membership with a half-price sale before reopening, using cable spots. The goal was to sell 200 memberships by the reopening date; that goal was reached two weeks in advance of the target date, and had been exceeded by the time of actual reopening.

Totem Lumber Company had previously used newspapers to advertise in its four different branch areas. The company added cable in the Lakes Cablevision area, tailoring a series of commercials to the interests of the rural lumberyard's customers. It subsequently went on record (with a videotaped testimonial) as saying that it had "never felt as much response from any other advertising media before."

The local (and only) appliance store in McHenry had been selling some 28 units a month before it started advertising on cable. Once the cable spots started running, sales increased to 108 units a month.

An established floor covering store in Grand Haven, Michigan, which had been using local newspapers, found that the day after it started its cable advertising nine people came into the store and said that they hadn't even known the store existed until they had seen the cable spot.

A car dealer in Auburn, Washington, saw his sales increase by 33 percent after running just $2,000 worth of local cable advertising.

Keating Ford of Stratford, Connecticut, ran a trial advertising package on Southern Connecticut Cablevision with a single commercial for Ford trucks and watched its truck sales triple. With additional spot buys and a second commercial (this one featuring cars and custom vans), new car and truck sales for the first two months of 1984 were up 87 percent over the same months in 1983, while the vans sold out. In both instances, the dealership president noted, adding cable was the only change that had been made in Keating's advertising.

Many of these stories came from the systems' relaying what advertisers told them. Sometimes, though, these success reports do not come to the system directly from the advertiser. One system told the story of a car dealer who came to it wanting to advertise on cable. He had made that decision after an elderly couple had come into his lot shopping for a car, and in the course of talking with him had said that before they made a decision, they would have to visit the competing car dealer they had seen advertising on the cable system, referring to that dealer by the name of the alter ego he assumed in his cable commercials.

Undoubtedly there will be local businesses that will still feel that they are too small to consider using cable. If yours is one of them, consider this. In Beacon, there is a little luncheonette tucked away on Main Street. It had never done any kind of advertising before and had a consistently moderate level of business. An account executive at U.S. Cablevision convinced the proprietors to place just one 30-second commercial a week on the system's local newscast. The day after the first spot ran, the luncheonette was packed with customers at lunchtime. That increase has been maintained since, and the owners say they have received lots of feedback from customers on their cable advertising.

Another Beacon restaurant that advertised on the system noted that although no one ever mentions its newspaper or radio ads, one out of ten customers inevitably comment on its cable commercials. This is in no way an isolated instance. Many advertisers from all over the country report similar behavior: People rarely acknowledge print or radio advertising, but they always say, "I saw you [your ad] on cable [TV]."

Sometimes ads can bring results of a somewhat unusual nature. For one car dealer, a fairly general spot was produced that included several shots panning over the dealer's used car lot. After the spot had been running for a few weeks, the dealer reports, a woman came into the showroom, asked if he still had a particular red car which she had noticed in one of those panning shots (he did), and bought that car.

And then of course there's the situation in which clients have called a system to say that they might have to cancel their cable advertising for the simple reason that they could not handle all the business it is bringing in.

Now obviously not every campaign can have these results, but the point is that cable advertising can be affordable, effective, and successful on the local level.

INTERCONNECTS AND REP FIRMS

In some instances, advertisers will need to cover geographic areas larger than those served by a single cable system. Depending upon the size of the area, an advertiser would have to place a commercial on anywhere from two to dozens of systems to achieve the desired coverage. Trafficking a buy of this order can be somewhat complicated; fortunately, the cable industry is developing two solutions to the problem: *interconnections* (usually called *interconnects*), and *sales representatives* (*rep firms*).

An interconnect exists where two or more cable systems link themselves together to distribute a programming signal simultaneously. The primary purpose of an interconnect is to maximize the effectiveness of an advertising schedule by offering a multiple-system buy in which only one contract need be negotiated. Interconnects can range from covering entire states to linking two small communities. The most rapid development in this area, though, is that designed to interconnect systems in and around major metropolitan areas.

Interconnects can be of two varieties, commonly known as *hard* and *soft* interconnects. Hard or "true" interconnects are those where systems are directly linked by cable or by microwave relays, and the signal is fed to the entire interconnect by one headend. Soft, "simulated", or "paper" interconnects have no direct operational connection between the participating systems. Instead, they are set up so that the same commercial is inserted simultaneously at each of the participating systems by use of videocassettes distributed to each system. Soft interconnects are usually run either by a cooperative effort among the systems or by an independent sales representative. These distinctions, however, are relevant only to the system operators; to the viewer or advertiser, there is no functional difference.

Sales representatives or rep firms are companies set up to represent systems for advertising in return for a sales commission. They serve their affiliated systems in several ways. First, they act as additional salespower for each system, or they may actually become the system's sales department. Second, rep firms encourage multiple-system buys because they make the advertiser's job easier by providing a single person to deal with in making those buys.

One advantage of interconnects to local advertisers is that it enables them to reach areas they might not have been able to reach economically with other media. One auto dealer in Illinois said he had been trying to expand his customer pull into several nearby towns for 14 years, but that the only way to do so had been by using prohibitively expensive newspaper advertising. After running spots on the cable interconnect in his area at a fraction of the print costs he might have incurred, he soon found himself with many customers from those previously untapped locations.

There is one problem, though, in buying across a large number of systems, be it through an interconnect or individual placement, and that is that with network rates as low as they are, it is possible to run into a situation where a regional spot can cost more than a national network spot. For example, when to cover 10 target areas you buy a total of 80 systems (or their equivalent) at an average rate of $25/spot/system (total cost $2,000/spot), it could turn out that the network in which you are buying the local avails is selling the same spot in the same time period for only $1,500.

Even so, it is quite likely that interconnects will become an important part of the cable advertising scene. Viacom president and CEO Terrence Elkes has commented that the Bay Area Interconnect, which covers the San Francisco–San Jose area with 37 cable systems (including Viacom's San Francisco system), may become an entity with sufficient coverage to parallel and compete with the San Francisco broadcast ADI/DMA.

SEVEN

COMMERCIAL CREATIVITY ON CABLE

Much of the discussion surrounding the development of cable as an advertising medium has dealt with the new creative opportunities cable offers. So far most advertisers have tended to use the same commercials used on conventional television for their cable buys. However, cable's specialized programming and less-structured formats allow for new creative approaches that advertisers are beginning to take advantage of.

Most television campaigns are built on commercials that are created without any consideration for the programming environment in which they will appear. This is because most conventional television programming is designed to reach the widest general audience and is bought by advertisers for that purpose. There are not enough special-appeal programming opportunities available on broadcast television to justify special creative approaches. Cable, with its targeted audiences and specialized programming, often makes it appealing for advertisers to create commercials that are in tune with programming environments and the audiences they attract.

Here are some examples:

In 1982 Kraft decided it wanted to promote its food products directly to the youth market that was not tuned in to its more standard commercial fare. It wanted a creative, contemporary approach that would be appealing to this demographic group and fit the cable programming environment in which it would appear. Enlisting the services of Foote, Cone & Belding, Kraft developed two 30-second spots that were quite different from anything they had done before. The first spot, "Rapper," featured a series of quick shots of Kraft products in use accompanied by a pseudo-funky soundtrack. The second one was similar but also used a pair of teenagers in "new wave" garb with a synthesizer-based sound-track. These were produced for use on MTV and USA's *Night Flight* and were sufficiently successful to warrant repeated use on these networks as well as elsewhere.

The same year, Campbell-Ewald produced a spot for Chevrolet that broke new ground in long-form commercials. This spot, which subsequently won a variety of awards, was a 90-second montage of bizarre images featuring brightly colored sets, oversized props, musclemen, shapely women, flashing neon, and, moving through it all, the Camaro Z-28. The images were combined with a loud rock soundtrack (vaguely based on the Rolling Stones' hit, "Shattered") featuring fragmentary lyrics about "shadows." The result was an exciting spot that was used not only on cable, but also in movie theaters. Shorter versions were extracted and used on network television, but with somewhat less impact. This commercial was later followed up by a futuristic 90-second spot for Corvette, full of bright lights, animation, and special effects. Again the longer length allowed time for the theme and visual effects to develop, with the resulting commercial becoming virtually an entertainment that held the viewer's attention.

These four spots were certainly innovative, and they deserve the attention they have received. Unfortunately, they also suffer from the same authenticity problem as do many commercials that have attempted to be "contemporary": they tend to look and sound like the products of well-meaning adults who are trying to imitate their teenage children. Some subsequent efforts at fitting spots into the music video environment have been more convincing.

In 1983, Miller Brewing introduced a 60-second spot which, while not made specifically for MTV, was clearly designed with MTV in mind. It featured a well-known rock band performing at a club party (looking similar in some respects to MTV's own annual New Year's Eve parties) singing the Miller jingle as arranged in the band's own style. The production looked like a well-made music video and even featured the same typefont overlay at the beginning to announce the band's name and the jingle's title that MTV uses to introduce its music videos. (The idea of tagging commercials like music videos has since been picked up by other advertisers, including Clairol and Archway Cookies.)

The ultimate integrated commercial of this nature, though, premiered on September 14, 1984, during the cablecast of the MTV Music Video Awards Show: A 90-second spot created by Kenyon & Eckhardt specifically for use on MTV and filmed in England by MGMMO, one of the world's leading music video production firms. It incorporated massive surreal sets (created by the designers of the science fiction film, *Blade Runner*), lots of smoke, dancers in punk garb and hairstyles, and a memorable soundtrack, all of which fit perfectly into the MTV environment. According to Glenn A. Northrop, car advertising manager for Chrysler, the effectiveness of the commercial was underscored in research with 18- to 25-year-olds. Although both the lyrics and the visuals intentionally avoided giving a detailed sales message, after viewing the commercial the test subjects specifically "recalled" many more features and characteristics of the car than had actually been presented to them. Additionally, the commercial received a rousing ovation from the audience of rock stars and music industry executives at the actual MTV awards show in New York, who were able to view it as it was being shown on the network.

For Hearst/ABC's Daytime network (a predecessor of Lifetime), Corning Glass prepared a series of three commercials, 3, 4, and 5 minutes long, respectively, in which Cornelius, the company's chef/spokesman, demonstrated to the interviewer/host the preparation of several dishes. In the process he showed how Corning Ware items could be used to great advantage in the preparation and storage of the foods. Each commercial ended by inviting the viewer to write to Corning for a recipe booklet featuring the dishes demonstrated in the spots.

The Sears Financial Network (Allstate, Dean Witter Reynolds, and Coldwell Banker) sponsored a series of five-minute infomercials called "Dollar Guide" that ran on the family-oriented CBN Cable Network. Produced in association with the USC Graduate Business School, these spots featured actor William Schallert narrating personal financial management advice segments. At the close of each spot, viewers were given an address to which to write for a transcript of that spot.

In some instances, cable gives an advertiser the opportunity to expand use of preexisting spots that have had limited runs in regular television outlets. For example, Anheuser-Busch has had a number of somewhat avant-garde (and expensive) television commercials made for Budweiser which were usable for *Saturday Night Live* or the very few other youth-oriented offerings on television, but not for the average football game. These spots have since run often on MTV and on USA's *Night Flight*.

LONG-FORM COMMERCIALS

The perpetual increase in television time and production costs have gradually forced advertisers into shorter and shorter commercial units. The result has been commercials created to fit into 30 seconds, even if more time would allow for a more creative sales message. As these costs continue to rise, some agencies have suggested that their clients try to sell more than one product in the same 30 seconds. With cable, the 30-second limit can be realistically expanded to 45, 60, 90, 120 seconds or longer to accommodate whatever length is needed to tell the complete product or service story. After all, many products do not lend themselves to the type of fast-paced hard sell characteristic of many 30-second spots; these include many high-priced items, or complex items where the consumer requires more information for the decision-making process than can be presented in 30 seconds.

There are three basic purposes for which long-form commercials are used. The first is simply to extend a message that could be presented in the standard 30-second length, though a better use would be to use the time to express or expand upon a message that might not work as well when squeezed into 30 seconds.

Two good examples of this are to be found in two more Budweiser commercials. One, called "Weekend," is a 90-second production showing people wrapping up their work weeks and partying Friday night in a bright and lively bar. It is made up of quick cuts and sight gags featuring young adults of various physical and social types; the soundtrack is a loud country-rock version of the Budweiser song without lyrics or dialogue. There is a

30-second version of this spot that plays well but doesn't have the time to set the mood and build the energy level that the longer one does. (The 90-second commercial has also gained a certain notoriety as the first spot where people actually drink the beer on screen, which cannot be done on broadcast television).

The other, called "Volunteers," is a human interest mini-drama. Running two minutes, it shows a farmer discovering a fire in his barn, his wife calling the fire department, and the various volunteer firefighters rushing from their regular jobs in town to put out the fire and save all the farm animals. The tension builds throughout until the fire is finally out and everyone relaxes on the farmhouse porch with bottles of Budweiser served by the grateful couple. This is an effective and watchable commercial that gives its story time to unfold at an appropriate pace that leads up to a natural connection between the story and the product.

Foote, Cone and Belding/Honig produced a 2-minute commercial for the State of Alaska Division of Tourism composed mostly of gorgeous scenic footage of Alaska's vacation areas, backed by a preexisting musical paean to the state. The variety and the beauty of the film had much greater impact over two minutes than it could have had in 30 seconds. This spot and the "Volunteers" spot were national finalists in the first CLIO competition that included categories for cable advertising.

Most direct-response commercials are two minutes long in order to demonstrate properly the product being sold and to show the ordering address and/or phone number for a long enough time for viewers to write it down. (Direct-response advertising will be covered in detail in Chapter 10.)

Of course, the original long-form commercial is the motion picture trailer, and several major studios have advertised films on cable by running the same two-minute trailer shown in theaters, as well as their regular 30-second television commercials.

A word of warning. If you are going to use more time, be sure you use it wisely. The ability to use long-form commercials represents an opportunity, not an obligation; if you have nothing significant to add, don't stretch a commercial just because the time is available. I have seen several commercials that ran 90 seconds or longer that could have gotten their messages across effectively in less time, and that become tedious, uninformative, and even irritating as they went on.

Nonstandard-length commercials (those not in multiples of 30 seconds) do not seem to have caught on yet in regular usage, since networks and systems cannot always fit them in neatly, but they have been used effectively. A few years ago Cox Cable of Jefferson Parish, Louisiana, was running a 45-second spot for a local health spa that worked quite well. Before you produce an odd-length spot, though, check in advance with the network(s) and/or system(s) you hope to run it on to make sure it will be accepted.

The second purpose is to combine a commercial message with some sort of program material. Most of these run 90 or 120 seconds, starting with a short teaser, followed by a 30-second commercial (often an existing television spot) and then the remainder of the program material. These tend to work best when the material used is compatible with the program environment.

Cable Health Network (the other predecessor of Lifetime) featured 90-second "Cable Health Breaks" structured along these lines. Among the participating advertisers were Aim and Crest toothpastes, which each sponsored dental care segments produced in cooperation with the American Dental Association, and Contac cold medicine, which sponsored a segment on how to handle children's colds. Lifetime has continued this series as "Lifetime Minutes" (the "minute" actually referring to the 60 seconds of editorial material accompanying the 30-second spot).

Noxzema sponsored a series of 90-second segments, entitled "Another Close Shave," which highlighted memorable sports contests that were won in their final moments. American Express presented a series of 2½-minute features called "Do You Know Me?" profiling major sports figures in a format complementary to its "Do You Know Me?" commercials. In these features, the athlete's achievements were shown and described in one and two minutes, respectively, of film/tape clips, although the name of the person saluted was not revealed until the end of the segment. In both series, which ran on ESPN, a standard 30-second television commercial for the sponsor was inserted about halfway through the program material.

No Nonsense pantyhose ran a similarly formatted series of fifty-two 90-second spots called "History . . . in the Company of Women," which featured 60-second profiles of remarkable women achievers throughout history, with a 30-second No Nonsense commercial inserted after the opening teaser.

In October 1984, General Foods began running a series of 2-minute spots called "Shortcuts" on five major cable networks. Each "Shortcut" consists of 90 seconds of informational material on such topics as shopping, entertaining, nutrition, and food preparation, with a standard 30-second commercial inserted after the opening teaser. With these commercials, General Foods is hoping to reach young, active consumers who are light viewers of regular broadcast television and whose busy lifestyles make them receptive to convenience foods and ideas to help them use them. Interestingly, the company is so determined that the "Shortcuts" be viewed as service announcements rather than as extended commercials that it does not use its own products in the information segments unless the subject matter specifically calls for their use.

The system can also work in shorter formats. In one 60-second spot, Procter & Gamble prefaced a standard 30-second television commercial for Crisco which featured Loretta Lynn as spokeswoman with a 30-second profile of the country music star. American Home Products did the same with another country singer, Charly McClain, for Luck's Beans.

The third purpose is to provide the consumer with more detailed information about a product or service than can be presented in a 30-second spot. Four steps are involved in a consumer's purchase decision process:

1. *Awareness.*   The consumer has to be made aware that the product or service in question exists and is available. As a rule, this is the one thing all commercials can provide.

2. *Comprehension of product characteristics.*   Here is where we begin to run into problems with most television advertising. The average 30-second spot simply isn't long enough to describe fully all the details of a product, much less go into how they can be used to the consumer's benefit. That's important, because the next step is

3. *Conviction.*   This develops when the consumer has been given sufficient information to decide whether the product is something he or she wants and can use (although in many instances the average consumer may consider these as mutually exclusive). This should, if all goes well, lead to

4. *Purchase.*

The lack of time pressure in cable can make a measurable difference in how companies present their products. For example, there was a significant difference between two ads for Swift's Sizzlean as designed for television and for cable. The 30-second TV spot used an exaggerated "slice of life" approach, with strips of bacon and Sizzlean magically flying through the air and unrealistic acting as a woman tells her doubting family why she is switching from the former product to the latter. For cable, though, Swift presented Sizzlean in one of a series of two-minute commercials called "Cooking Easy." In this spot, Nancy [Nancy Rodriquez, a Swift home economist] shows in detail the various differences between Sizzlean and bacon, the different cuts of meat they come from, and how that results in the leanness and lower shrinking factor of Sizzlean. She goes on to demonstrate how to properly cook Sizzlean and how to create various dishes using it, in the process demonstrating how two strips of Sizzlean replace three strips of bacon for these purposes. Finally, she identifies a variety of women's magazines (whose cover logos are shown on screen) in which store coupons for Sizzlean can be found.

There have been over two dozen other "Cooking Easy" two-minute commercials featuring Nancy (including another version of the Sizzlean one). In one for Swift International Frozen Entrees, she shows how Swift prepares several of these dishes before packaging them, then gives tips on how to cook and serve them. For Soup Starter, an instant soup mix, Nancy demonstrates how fruits and vegetables can be dehydrated (for example, how grapes can be turned into raisins) as a preface to showing how Soup Starter's ingredients are simply natural dehydrated vegetables, pasta, and stock to which one adds water and simmers to create fresh homemade soup. She also shows how Soup Starter can be prepared in advance in a crockpot if one is pressed for time. For Butterball turkey, there are commercials showing how to shop for a turkey and how to cook one.

Although two minutes can often suffice, there are situations where you might need more than that in order to convey the message. Many products are best sold by demonstrations rather than by rapid and/or limited listing of their features. This is where the infomercial comes in.

INFOMERCIALS

The term *infomercial* has attained great currency in the cable area. By definition, the infomercial is designed to give the viewer information about the product (or service) being offered and its uses, often combined with other related information. While in general usage the word has come to imply a commercial length of 3 to 8 minutes, properly speaking any commercial that offers a product in an informational setting can be called an infomercial. That goes for such commercials as a 3-minute spot showing how aluminum foil can be used in making and wrapping ornamental Christmas cookies, a 7½-minute spot featuring the president of a shoe company demonstrating to a couple the features and durability of a newly developed work shoe, or even a 60-second commercial showing how to make napkin rings out of toilet tissue and spray paint. The "Cooking Easy" spots are just as much infomercials as the Corning Ware commercials discussed earlier.[1]

Through the use of infomercials, you have the ability to present potential customers with all the information they need and you want them to have about a product or service. The infomercial can also serve to fill gaps in the information link between you and your customer, particularly where you are not directly involved with the selling process. Manufacturers usually have to depend on retail stores to sell their goods, and most of the time the consumer cannot depend on the store clerk to provide information about products. This is especially true as the retail trend turns from specialty stores to high-volume discount, catalog, or department stores, where employees often are not equipped to do much more than retrieve merchandise from the stockroom and ring up the sale

---

[1]Infomercials should not be confused with *advertorials*. While some people use the terms interchangeably, an advertorial is really a paid commentary by a company relating to a situation rather than selling a product. For example, a 5-minute spot demonstrating how to give your car a tune-up using Mobil Oil products would be considered an infomercial; Mobil's series of "Fables For Our Time," which used animated animal stories to present in parable form the company's viewpoints on government regulation of energy companies, were advertorials. Corporate image advertisements or public service ads sponsored by corporations are not really in either category.

on the register. In research on infomercials, several test group members specifically pointed out that they found the infomercials more valuable in answering questions about products than were store clerks.

One thing to keep in mind is that the point of an infomercial is to provide information, not to overwhelm the viewer with razzle-dazzle or nonstop plugging. The viewer must have the idea that he or she is getting useful and factual information; it is not the place for hyperbole. Ideally, you should find a relatively "down-to-earth" spokesperson who won't overwhelm the message; if you can find someone from within your own company to serve the purpose (and it doesn't have to be the president), so much the better. A celebrity spokesperson can be used, but not at the expense of believability. Most viewers may recognize a celebrity, but they also have to believe that he or she possesses knowledge or experience that qualifies him or her to speak for the company or its product. Besides, in many cases company spokespersons may become celebrities in their own right from appearing in commercials, which makes them more valuable for appearances at trade shows and sales meetings, not to mention consumer-targeted promotions.

Concentrate on the information being disseminated, and how the product relates to it. If you are conducting what is basically a product demonstration, make sure the examples show realistic and practical uses; it is to your advantage if you can also show or state some uses that might not be immediately evident to the viewer. If you are presenting a more instructional type of show, show clearly how the product can be used in connection with the matter at hand, without an overt sales pitch.

Another consideration is that, particularly where several different ideas, such as recipes, are developed during the spot, you can't expect viewers to remember all the information or to think to take notes (should they wish to) before it's too late. Also, some of the ideas may not be of immediate interest to a particular viewer, yet he or she cannot be sure that the infomercial will be repeated just when he or she is thinking, "Gee, if I could only remember that idea I saw in that commercial; boy, would that help me now!" This is one reason why it is recommended that you include some form of direct-response device by which viewers can obtain further information on what has been discussed in the infomercial, whether it be a booklet or catalog they can send or call for, a hot-line telephone number they can call to have questions answered, and/or a means to order the product in question if you intend to sell it directly.

There is one possible disadvantage to extended infomercials. Because of their length, some people feel that their impact and interest fade quickly, perhaps even after one viewing, although there is some disagreement about this.

Do infomercials really work? Are they worth the time and effort necessary to create and use them? These are among the questions being researched through a unique cable network called The Cableshop. The Cableshop is a venture of Adams-Russell, an electronics company that also operates cable systems. It offers cable subscribers two or more channels on which the programming is comprised entirely of long-form infomercials. These spots are scheduled to run continuously and the channels may be viewed at any time, but the subscriber also has the option of calling up specific messages on demand by so instructing the Cableshop system computer by telephone. The initial test of The Cableshop was launched in 1982 in Peabody, Massachusetts, a suburb of Boston selected because it was considered to be a "typical American town," as well as one in which Adams-Russell owned and operated the cable system. The service was continued in Peabody in 1983 and introduced in a half-dozen other markets around the country to a quarter-million subscribers that fall, with additional expansion planned for the future.

The results of the original 1982 Cableshop test disclosed some encouraging facts about consumer reaction to infomercials. Over a nine-month period:

> 70 percent of viewers found the long-form infomercials run on The Cableshop more interesting than network television commercials; 51 percent of regular Cableshop viewers found the infomercials more interesting than network television *programs.*
>
> 85 percent of viewers said the infomercials provided them with useful information (37 percent found them very or extremely useful), twice the number who found network television commercials at all useful.
>
> 50 percent of viewers said they had a more favorable attitude toward the participating advertisers after viewing their infomercials. (It has been suggested that infomercials are designed to

create a bond of trust, as opposed to 30-second spots designed to make an impression on the viewer.)

30 percent indicated they would respond to an infomercial, and nearly a third of those said they had already taken action ranging from requesting further information to actually purchasing the advertiser's product or service.

A survey conducted in January 1984 by Polaris Research Associates over the six markets in which The Cableshop had been introduced showed even better results. Thirty-five percent of Cableshop viewers had watched 7 or more infomercials in the preceding month, and of those who had seen specific infomercials, 83 percent were aware of the products shown, 63 percent had a positive attitude toward the advertisers, 50 percent intended to buy one or more of the products, and 37 percent had actually made a recent purchase. Each of these figures (which are averages based on a test of 14 infomercials) were significantly higher than comparable ones for viewers who had not seen the infomercials in question.

HOME SHOPPING

The Cableshop is just one part of a larger field known as home shopping. As the term implies, the intent is to allow the consumer to shop from home. The differences in specific forms of home shopping cluster around the various definitions of the verb "to shop." In some instances, it means to make a purchase; in others, simply to gather information for decision-making purposes, not necessarily culminating in a purchase at that time. Over the years there have been a number of programs of both types on the national and local level, such as *The Shopping Game, The Good Buy Bazaar, The Sharper Image Living Catalog, Viewmart, The Cable Store,* and *Shopper's Guide of the Air.* Most of these had limited runs, whether by design (some were strictly experimental in nature) or circumstance. Probably the best known of these ventures, and one that is still running, is *The Home Shopping Show.*

Originally created in Chicago in 1979 and marketed as a local program, *The Home Shopping Show* was later picked up for national distribution and subsequently bought outright by the Modern Satellite Network. Although it has been through several changes of hosts, sets, and format, the basic concept remains that of a talk show whose guests are representatives of companies who have stopped by to discuss their products and/or subjects related to them. There are usually three major segments of about 8 minutes each, sometimes with breaks between segments that feature shorter (30- to 120-second) infomercials. I picked a show at random, and here is what that show featured:

Following the title sequence that previewed all three of the show segments, the first segment discussed reducing home energy costs with insulation. Joe Kimpflan of CertainTeed Home Institute (sponsor of the segment) outlined how insulation reduces heat loss in homes, and host Bob Jones demonstrated the ease of installing CertainTeed insulation in an attic. Kimpflan told of a rebate promotion being offered by the company, and the segment ended with a tag inviting viewers to write or phone for free brochures and information about the rebate offer.

The second segment was co-sponsored by the Georgia Peanut Commission and DuPont. It featured Marilyn Hubert of the Georgia Peanut Commission showing a variety of dishes made with peanuts and singing the praises of bakeware coated with Silverstone for nonstick preparation of same. She also prepared two cookie recipes on camera and showed how baked goods packed in festive baskets can make attractive gifts. The segment was tagged with an offer for cookbooks published by GPC and by DuPont.

The final segment was sponsored by The Bradford Exchange, a company serving essentially as a commodities exchange for collectibles. Harriet DeLasky, VP-brokerage operations, discussed the history of decorative plates and plate collecting, while showing a selection of both antique and currently available plates and describing what services The Bradford Exchange performs for collectors. The segment closed with a 2-minute direct-response commercial for a $19 decorative plate featuring Little Orphan Annie and Sandy (from the Broadway and movie musical, *Annie*).

The show closed with a repetition of the three offers made during it and an invitation for viewers to write to MSN with their comments (in return for which the network sends out a small MSN premium).

Although most shows feature three different sponsored segments, sponsors can also purchase an entire show, as the Soap and Detergent Association (SDA) did. In this two-part show, the hosts talked with Dr. V. William Greene, professor of public health and microbiology at the University of Minnesota, about the history of the use of soap and detergents (a fairly recent development) and the effects this has had on society and human welfare, and with Mildred Gallik, director of consumer affairs of the SDA, about how soaps and detergents should be used. Breaks were taken in the show during which public service announcements from the SDA were run, and at the end of the show there was an offer for viewers to request a series of SDA pamphlets.

Probably one of the best examples of a well-made and effective infomercial I've seen is a segment from an October 1981 *Home Shopping Show* for the Black & Decker "Dust Buster" hand-held vacuum cleaner and "Stowaway" folding stepstool. The simple demonstrations of the operation of these devices, together with the casual conversation between the show's hostess and the Black & Decker representative regarding possible uses around the home for each product, were far more effective in illustrating the products' advantages than were the standard 30-second television commercials for them. The cost of the infomercial: $7,000 for production and five airings. The cost just to produce the 30-second spot for the "Dust Buster" alone: over $70,000.

According to Robert Finehout, VP-programming for MSN, the sponsorship rates for *The Home Shopping Show* have remained fairly consistent at $11,000 for an 8-minute segment, and $29,000 for the full 28-minute show. This includes production and five network runs. For a slight additional talent cost, sponsors may use tapes of their segments in other venues, such as point-of-purchase and dealer training.

Opportunities for home shopping programming are by no means limited to the network level. Several cable systems also offer some form of home shopping activity; one of the most successful has been the Home Shopping Channel on Village Cable of Chapel Hill, North Carolina. This is a dedicated channel on which the system gives advertisers the chance to run half-hour programs providing consumer information. As of October 1984, the time charge for a half-hour show was $40 a run, with a minimum of 12 runs a month. Production costs average $250 to $500 a show.

Probably the best-known shown on the channel is the *Woofer & Tweeter Consumer Electronics Show*, run by a local stereo store. Each month the show presents tips on how to shop for, select, and maintain audio and video equipment. While the four segments in each show are separated by standard broadcast commercials for specific major audio equipment manufacturers (with appropriate store tags), the segments themselves rarely try to sell anything except in an infomercial format. The owner of the Woofer & Tweeter store, Ed Jenkins, reports that literally hundreds of people have come into his store and commented (mostly favorably) on the show, as well as bought equipment.

Also on the Home Shopping Channel is *Projects Unlimited,* a half-hour show aimed at the do-it-yourselfer, which each month shows how to make a different home improvement or renovation (building a deck, adding on storm windows and doors, and so on). The show is presented by Fitch Lumber Company of Carrboro, North Carolina. Other shows on the channel have included mall fashion shows; general tours interviewing groups of merchants within a shopping center; and a music-oriented talk show featuring local artists, run by a music store.

One popular form of home shopping show involves literally "home shopping," or shows about real estate. The Home Shopping Channel carried a series on how to buy a house, hosted by a real estate agent who interviewed real estate agents, mortgage bankers, and other people one is likely to deal with in the course of shopping for and buying a house. In Westchester County, New York, former Grey Advertising VP Jack Waite produces a show called *The House Hunter,* which not only shows individual houses and the names and phone numbers of the brokers selling them, but also gives minitours of the communities in which they are located. Marje Fogel Communications produces a similar program focusing on new condominium development in the greater New York City area. CPI of Louisville, Kentucky (now known as Dimension Cable), had an entire 24-hour channel devoted to selling homes and providing information to homeowners on topics such as decorating, remodeling, and energy conservation, while NYT Cable TV in Audubon, New Jersey, has a weekly show, sponsored and hosted by a local broker, that reviews current real estate news and offerings in the southern New Jersey area.

PRODUCTION TIPS

One of the keys to taking advantage of cable's creative opportunities is knowing how to be creative on a budget. In a world where a 30-second television commercial usually costs tens or hundreds of thousands of dollars to produce, it is now possible to make commercials for a tiny fraction of those sums using good planning and imagination.

I want to point out that this section is just as applicable for the small advertiser working on a local system level as for the larger national advertiser. In fact, many of these ideas were developed by cable systems producing spots for their local clients, as well as by agencies working for the leading national advertisers on cable. Many of the cable systems accepting advertising are equipped to produce high-quality commercials at generally reasonable costs scaled to the budgets of local advertisers. They usually have professional-grade equipment, and some have special-effects generators of various capabilities that can be used to manipulate the shape and position of the images on the screen. These features can be used to animate slides, photographs, or artwork to create lively commercials from static material, as well as to highlight regular film or tape material.

• *Do adequate preproduction planning.* I cannot emphasize this point too strongly as a factor in efficient production and cost management. By planning just what you intend to get on film or on tape (which is usually a lot faster and cheaper), the amount of time wasted in having to make decisions on the set is reduced. Don't stifle your director's creativity, but try to help him or her work out as many shots as possible in advance. "Editing in the camera" can help minimize the need for extra takes and expensive postproduction editing.

One factor often overlooked in planning is *where* to produce the spot. Many national advertisers using large advertising agencies find that while some price-shopping is done among individual production facilities, they still end up choosing from resources in the most expensive markets—New York, Chicago, and Los Angeles. Advertisers and agencies who have the flexibility to travel should consider looking further afield. Substantial cost savings can be achieved by shooting in places like Dallas, Portland, St. Louis, Phoenix, Miami, Cincinnati, and other cities that have as good facilities and people as can be found in the larger cities.

The simpler the production requirements, the greater number of suitable facilities there are to choose from, but even very complex commercials can be made at reduced cost. The Plymouth Duster spot discussed earlier actually cost 10 to 25 percent *less* to film in England than if it had been done in the U.S.

• *Shoot more than one commercial at a time.*   If you plan to make more than one spot for your campaign, see if you can do so during the same shoot. The incremental costs of using a studio or remote unit and crew for additional time at a session are far less than having to reassemble those resources for separate tapings. Again, you can deal with this in your planning stages. The 90-second Chevrolet cable spots described earlier were a result of this kind of planning; when I asked the people at Campbell-Ewald what those commercials cost to make, I was told that they couldn't really break out the cost for the 90-second versions, since they were created as parts of production packages that filmed a lot of generic footage to be assembled into various commercials (specifically, a 90-, a 60- and two 30-second spots). It was, however, only the ability to make such extensive use of the footage shot that made these expensive (around $600,000 each) productions practical. Similarly, many infomercial series have had all their new footage taped in single sessions.

If you can edit more than one commercial while you have access to an editing facility, you can probably save money as well. The key is using the resources at hand as fully as possible. I would also suggest retaining all usable outtake footage (anything that isn't spoiled, damaged, or otherwise completely unscreenable) rather than leaving it on the cutting-room floor, since another way to cut costs is to:

• *Use existing material.*   It is not always necessary to shoot new footage to create cable commercials. In many instances, you can take advantage of existing material, especially when trying to produce long-form commercials on a limited budget. For example, J. Walter Thompson U.S.A. created a two-minute spot for Kawasaki motorcycles by cutting together existing film clips and adding a new musical soundtrack. Total cost: $5,000. The same agency also created several 90-second spots for Kraft by using material from various television commercials and outtakes accumulated over the years.

For The Cableshop, Eastman Kodak took advantage of the library of films produced by its photography information division to create 11 different infomercials, for which it added new soundtracks and filmed tags offering two pamphlets.

Corporate films are not only a good source of usable commercial footage, but can also be used as cable programming in their own right. A series of specials shown periodically over SPN called *How's Business* has been produced by American Express using footage drawn from its bimonthly employee communications videotape program, *On Location*. Several companies have experimented with using cable as a means to communicate with stockholders and/or employees based in various locations around the country (see page 75). I am not necessarily talking about annual reports here. Each year, the Kemper Insurance Company sponsors a golf tournament which is covered by one of the major television networks, and produces a film of tournament highlights that is subsequently distributed to the company's agents for showing at schools, to civic organizations, and over local television stations. Starting in 1982, to attract attention to each year's tournament, the company has sponsored showings of the film of the prior year's event on ESPN.

Some production houses and cable systems have produced what are called *generic commercials*. These spots usually present a general theme of visual elements to which you can add your own script or use a standard script supplied with the tape. The advantage of these spots is that they tend to be of high technical and visual quality. The problem is that they are, of necessity, a little too generalized to have any significant impact. Sometimes one really is hard-pressed to make a realistic connection between the commercial and the advertiser.

Some production houses also produce reels of "production elements," usually animated titles or special effects that can be used by a variety of businesses but are beyond the ordinary technical and/or budgetary limitations of the system and/or advertiser. These elements can be edited into a spot in the same way sound effects and stock music (which may also be available with the visual elements) can be.

Advertisers who use or have used radio will generally have radio commercials that can be used as the basis for cable commercials. By adding video, the impact of the radio commercial can often be greatly enhanced (Stan Freberg's legendary "aural pictures" radio spots for RAB notwithstanding). If the radio commercial has been running prior to or at the same time as its video counterpart, the cable commercial will have the added advantage of a soundtrack familiar to the viewer.

• *Explore additional uses for infomercials or long-form commercials.* You can amortize production costs over a wider basis if the commercials have uses outside cable. Some advertisers have already used their infomercials as point-of-purchase films in retail outlets and for internal sales training and motivation, directly and/or through distributors around the country.

• *Use simple sets.* In many cases, you do not need elaborate sets, especially if the focus is on a product or service rather than on staging a production number. You may find, particularly with retail businesses, that the place of business itself is a good place to do a location shoot.

• *Think professional.* As a rule, it helps to try to make your spot look as professional as possible. By professional, I do not necessarily mean slick or expensive; it's just that more attention can be paid to a message when the viewer is not distracted by obvious flaws such as sloppy camerawork, fuzzy sound, or talent who mispronounce words.

• *Be creative.* There's no real substitute for ingenuity and creativity; not only do neither of them have to be expensive, they are often the best way of keeping costs down. On the local level, several cable systems have spoken of producing jewelry store commercials using only a pair of hands and a ring against some black velvet, at a cost of as little as $40. Another common format for budget spots is having one person on camera silently reacting to an off-screen announcer. Many systems have reported their average production charges for a 30-second commercial at $150 to $300 (and it is not uncommon for some to discount or waive production costs as part of an advertising package buy), and I have seen many spots created at those prices that looked quite good.

Here are a few examples of local commercials that were creative in their concept, copy, execution, and/or use of limited resources:

Sully's Irish Pub in Peoria Heights, Illinois, came up with the idea for the spot that it ran on General Electric Cablevision's Peoria system. The idea was to do a takeoff on the popular Miller

Lite Beer advertising campaign in which sports figures argue over whether "less filling" or "tastes great" is the brew's most attractive quality. In the Sully's spot, Dick Versace, "Famous Coach" (of the Bradley Braves, a local college basketball team that went on to become NIT champions later that year), debated with Jack Brickhouse, "Famous Announcer" (the former WGN-TV announcer for the Chicago Cubs), over whether they go to Sully's for the "food and drink" or the "atmosphere and entertainment." The discussion is broken up by Pete Vonachen, "Famous Restaurateur" (the proprietor of another Peoria restaurant unrelated to Sully's) who, like Marv Throneberry in the Miller commercials, says he doesn't know why he was asked to appear in the spot. This commercial ran not only on cable, but also on a Peoria television station during an NBC sports show, and a feature article about it appeared in a local newspaper.

Uptown Shopping Center in Des Moines, Iowa, pooled the limited advertising resources of its tenants by making a series of four commercials promoting both itself and the individual businesses. Each spot featured pictures of each of four different storefronts within the shopping center, with a headshot of the proprietor or manager superimposed in the corner of the screen as the off-screen announcer read a brief sales pitch for that business. As a result, the production cost absorbed by each tenant was almost negligible.

A commercial for American Office Supply in Waco, Texas, opened with a businessman barking into his phone that he needs "legal pads, pens, and file folders, and I need them *fast!*" No sooner are the words out of his mouth than the items drop from above onto his desk. The rest of the commercial is a fairly routine sales message, pointing out that the advertiser doesn't deliver quite that fast, but usually can supply orders the same day from its complete stock of a wide selection of office supply needs. It ends with the same businessman wearing a hard hat and hesitantly saying into the phone, "Hello, uh, American Office Supply? I need, uh, a file cabinet," while nervously looking up toward the ceiling.

EIGHT

SPONSORSHIPS, TIE-INS, AND ADVERTISER-PRODUCED CABLE PROGRAMMING

In the so-called golden ages of radio and television, it was common for programs to be sponsored by individual advertisers. In many cases these advertisers had their agencies create and produce shows to order for them, and client identification with the program was a major factor. Often the client's name was part of the show's title, such as *The Bell Telephone Hour, Kraft Music Hall,* or even the somewhat unwieldy (but true) *Your Kaiser-Frazer Dealer Presents "Kaiser-Frazer Adventures in Mystery" Starring Betty Furness in "By-Line."* As television time became more expensive, exclusive sponsorship was replaced by selling time slots within the programs to several different advertisers. For a long time, most of these slots were 60 seconds long, but they gradually gave way to the now-dominant 30-second spots, and with a very few exceptions the concept of sole sponsorship drifted into history.

With the advent of cable as a programming medium (as opposed to a signal carrier), the opportunity to sponsor and develop shows has made a comeback, and not just on a network level. With cable's low cost and its willingness to accept new programming ideas, the field is now wide open for the would-be show sponsor/creator. Let's look at some examples of advertiser-produced and/or -sponsored programs that have appeared on cable to date.

67

One of the major announcements in the cable industry in 1981 was the decision by Bristol-Myers to commit $40 million over the next ten years to the USA Cable Network for the purpose of underwriting a weekly health-and-fitness series called *Alive and Well*. In exchange for underwriting the production and advertising costs, Bristol-Myers receives all the available advertising time for its own use. The show has proved quite popular and has even generated a quarterly magazine spinoff in which Bristol-Myers is also the sole advertiser.

Another Bristol-Myers sponsorship is the WTBS *Bristol-Myers Theatre*. This is a series of popular vintage movies, presented with limited commercial interruptions (all Bristol-Myers spots, of course). An interesting twist to this particular series is that each month, during one of the commercial breaks, viewers are presented with a selection of three film titles; they can then vote by telephone for which film they would like to see the following month. With an initial response of 5,000 calls in December 1981 and 19,000 the following month, WTBS was receiving over 30,000 calls a month by October 1983, a level that has been maintained since then.

Another sponsored offering on WTBS is *WomanWatch*, a series focusing on contemporary women's achievements and concerns. This show was created by BBDO for its client, Campbell Soup Company. Interestingly, BBDO does very little spot buying in cable, preferring to concentrate on developing suitable cable programs for its clients.

Tandy Corporation (parent company of Radio Shack) sponsored a series of half-hour programs on Financial News Network called *Technology Today*. Tandy produced the program, which was essentially a guide to computers and computing for the non-technically-minded businessperson, and had all the advertising time therein.

Nikon sponsors a series called *The Photographer's Eye*, which runs nationally on Satellite Program Network. The program features discussions with professional photographers about their styles and techniques. Nikon's participation in the series includes a 4-minute segment in each show demonstrating Nikon's professional photographic equipment, a corporate image spot produced especially for the series discussing the company's involvement with the space shuttle program, and a direct-response offer for its amateur photography magazine, *Nikon World.*

Procter & Gamble has probably been the advertiser most active in sponsoring programs, many created especially for it. Among the network series its products sponsor are *At Home with Beverly Nye; Cleaning Up Your Act; Mommy, Daddy and Me; Good Housekeeping's The Better Way;* and *Infants and Toddlers.*

Since 1980 Mazda Motors has sponsored the daily half-hour *Sports Look* series on USA Cable Network. Other sponsored shows on USA have included *Scholastic Sports Academy* (Kellogg's), *Coed* (Noxell), and two more Procter & Gamble series, *Cover Story* and *The Great American Homemaker.*

On Cable News Network, Lanier has been the prime (but not sole) sponsor of *Inside Business,* a Sunday evening interview show with corporate chief executives, with product exclusivity in the show. The Ford division of Ford Motor Company has a standing arrangement to sponsor all telecasts of presidential news conferences on CNN. When a news conference is announced by the White House, the network's traffic department automatically programs in a sponsor billboard prior to the start of the conference, and a 30-second Ford spot is shown between the conclusion of the conference and the start of the CNN analysis session that follows it.

Coverage of some sports events on ESPN have been made possible only because of sponsorship or underwriting by advertisers. In many cases this involves full coverage of sports that might receive only minimal excerpted coverage by the television networks, such as golf tournaments, track meets, and polo matches, and that would be too expensive for ESPN to produce on its own. Chrysler, Ford, and Rolex are among the advertisers that have participated in this manner.

Anheuser-Busch has taken several sponsorships on Black Entertainment Television, including two music shows (*Bud Video Soul* and *Michelob Black Showcase*), a sports talk show (*Bud Sports Rap*), and a weekly football MVP award, as well as being a major spot buyer in BET's sports coverage.

Fashion and fashion photography have been the subject of several special programs sponsored by leading retailers. In 1983 Saks Fifth Avenue sponsored a 60-minute special on USA Cable Network called *How to Make the Best of You,* a spinoff of the network's *You!* series. Program and commercial content over-lapped here as one feature of the show was a behind-the-scenes look at photo sessions in Mexico for the store's *Folio* catalog, while one of the four commercials produced by Saks for the show was a direct-response offering of the catalog (the other spots dealt with specific wardrobes and accessories). Later in the year, Sears presented *Pretty Pictures (The Wishbook on Location)* as a half-hour special on MSN which showed viewers how fashion photography is planned and created, with a behind-the-scenes look at photo sessions in Florida for the Sears catalog.

It is not necessary to be a major advertiser to sponsor a show on cable. In fact, it can even be easier for the smaller company. When I interviewed Palmer Cablevision (Naples, Florida) for the first set of CAB/Cable System Advertising Profiles, I found that much of its local programming had been created in response to specific advertiser needs. The system had been successfully selling advertising time on CNN and USA and on its own local news program. Sometimes, though, it ran into situations where either the programs were sold out or where the prospective advertiser felt that the particular programming wasn't quite the right environment for his or her ad. In many instances, the system's response was to come up with a new program based around the advertiser's interest—a gardening show for a local nursery, a golfing tips show for a local sporting goods dealer, and so on.

Purity Supreme, a supermarket chain in the Boston area, was one of two sponsors of a locally produced cable series called *The Chef's Kitchen,* starring a well-known chef from the area demonstrating recipes. During one of the commercial breaks in each show, Purity ran one of four 2-minute infomercials featuring the same chef talking with the managers of the meat, fish, produce, and consumer relations departments, respectively, about what the chain offered customers and what they should look for when shopping to get the best quality and values.

An interesting followup to this story is that the Boston-based Nabisco Confections company was so impressed with this local show that it had the producers tape four special episodes for it in which the chef demonstrated ways to use the various Nabisco candies in baking and entertaining. Nabisco published a booklet with the recipes and offered it free to viewers. These shows ran nationally over Modern Satellite Network with Nabisco sponsorship, and the company received requests for the recipe booklet from viewers in all 50 states.

If you produce your own show, take note of the fact that not only are these shows often much less expensive to produce for cable than for regular television (an entire cable series can cost less to produce than a single broadcast television commercial), but that the final costs can end up being still lower, since there may be an aftermarket for your show beyond its cable run. International distribution, domestic syndication, home videotape or videodisc, or internal use by way of in-store or dealer exhibition are among the possibilities to be considered.

It isn't always necessary, though, to create a whole new program. Take a look at existing local and network offerings. It may be attractive and advantageous to you to sponsor an existing program simply by buying all the available advertising time. Sponsorship can also provide a certain amount of ancillary benefits. To begin with, full sponsorship is the simplest way to guarantee product exclusivity within a show (although where possible, systems and networks do try to accommodate such requests, even for scatter-plan buys). In many situations you may find that there are volume discounts available in purchasing the advertising time. On top of that, it is likely that you can receive additional billboard mentions during the show's credits, such as "[Show] is brought to you by. . . ." In certain programs, it may also be possible to have some form of sponsor identification presented within the programming. This doesn't necessarily mean that in the middle of an entertainment show your logo will be hanging in back of the performers (though that's between you and whoever's producing the show); however, if you are sponsoring coverage of a local football game, it might be reasonable to expect to be able to have a banner with your company's name on it somewhere on the sidelines that will be visible on screen when the play moves in front of it.

You can also use your own creativity to come up with tie-ins for particular programming appropriate to your product or service. After the aforementioned Bristol-Myers/USA Network *Alive and Well* deal, the big sponsorship story in 1981 was the $20 million Timex/ESPN deal. In this situation not only did Timex purchase a long-term network spot schedule, but it was also named as official timekeeper for ESPN. In other, less elaborate deals,

Bulova became the official timepiece of Cable News Network and Seiko that of Satellite News Channel (and later of CNN), with their names appearing with on-screen time displays.

SEGMENT SPONSORSHIP

On a smaller scale, some advertisers find it attractive to sponsor specific segments of or features on programs. Over a period of time, this has the advantage not only of providing the sponsor with a less expensive suitable vehicle for a message, but also with viewer identification. For example, Mobil Oil has sponsored a "Player of the Week" award on Black Entertainment Television, and Owens-Corning an "Unsung Hero" feature on ESPN which each week recognizes outstanding achievements by high school athletes selected from nominations received from school coaches around the country.

The Weather Channel has raised segment sponsorship to a fine art, carrying a large number of advertisers who sponsor specific weather reports based on the conditions being reported. Here are some examples:

> Gatorade thirst quencher and Kool-Aid soft drink each sponsor "Heat Wave Alerts."
>
> Quaker Oats hot cereal sponsors "Cold Wave Alerts."
>
> Ski reports are sponsored by Maxwell House coffee and by American Motors, whose Eagle is the official car of the U.S. Ski Patrol.
>
> Anco windshield products sponsors precipitation forecasts.
>
> Bounce antistatic fabric softener sponsors the Bounce Static Report (indoor relative humidities).
>
> Prudential-Bache Securities sponsors agricultural reports that include not only weather reports of interest to farmers, but also the most recent closing commodities prices on the Chicago Board of Trade.

Each sponsored report is prefaced by an advertiser billboard announcement, and the sponsor's logo is on screen throughout the segment. The actual commercial follows or bisects the report.

In several cases, The Weather Channel has worked closely with advertisers to develop suitable features and commercials.

Some reports were added or revamped to relate to sponsoring products, and the network has even produced the commercials for some sponsors.

For DuPont's fibers division and Pant-her women's clothes, the network added a "Dress for the Weather" segment, reporting the forecast for the next 24 to 36 hours. It also filmed the commercial for Pant-her (which had never used television before and so had no previously made spots) showing how clothes made of DuPont polyester Dacron were fashionable and suitable for all kinds of weather.

For Ralston Purina pet foods, a feature called "Weatherize Your Pet" was developed in conjunction with the company's Purina brand group, its staff veterinarian, and its advertising agency. The network taped a series of 30-second infomercials giving tips on how to care for pets in various seasons (insulating doghouses, preventing hypothermia and frostbite, not leaving pets in closed cars in warm weather).

For Shell Oil, a series of weather safety tips was taped, showing how to protect oneself from hazardous conditions (tornadoes, lightning, floods) while traveling or vacationing.

In each of these cases, the network used its own on-air meteorologists as the commercial talent, which helped to further the identification of the sponsor with the program content.

Segment sponsors on Financial News Network have included Compaq Computers ("Market Movers Report"), Avis ("Business & Travel Weather"), Sanyo ("Business Week Outlook & Index Report"), and, of course, several major brokerage firms, including Shearson Lehman/American Express (daily bond reports), Merrill Lynch, and Dean Witter. A number of major West Coast metal traders have also created pseudo-sponsorships of some of FNN's commodities reports by regularly buying the adjacencies.

On Black Entertainment Television, AT&T and IBM each sponsor several editions of "Front Page," a two-minute weekday evening news update, and the various divisions of Ford Motor Company each sponsor two-minute "Minority Business Profiles" on a rotating basis.

Cable News Network has created several segments for advertisers, including a nightly "Tokyo Business Report" for Ricoh and NEC, air travel advisories for TraveLodge and Sheraton hotels, personal finance segments for Toyota, and nutrition segments for the Florida Department of Citrus and Total cereal. Other regular segment sponsors have included Duracell ("High-Tech House"), Bristol-Myers ("News from Medicine"), Dodge (economic updates), and Carnation, Kal-Kan, General Foods, Alpo, and Ralston Purina (pet care segments).

PROMOTION

In addition to the on-screen exposure advantages of program sponsorship, there is often a wide variety of opportunities for in-store merchandising and other related promotion. Ray Klinge of Satellite Program Network has pointed out the need for advertisers to make an effort to promote the programming they sponsor in order to help generate a larger audience for it. This can include running promotional spots on other services, running ads in program guides or other print media, using direct-mail inserts, placing counter cards or posters in any place(s) of business that get walk-in traffic, and generating press or other publicity. Where possible, such activities should be localized to individual systems.

A national retail store chain sponsoring a cable network series might place a general ad for the show in a national publication with a "Check your local cable system listings for time and channel" tag, and provide each of its stores with similar materials to be used in local media and in the store itself that can be customized to include "Mondays and Wednesdays at 8 P.M. on cable channel 24." An airline sponsoring a show could provide travel agencies with easeled cards that sit on agents' desks, or a travel agency taking local sponsorship of a show can have similar cards made up for itself. Any of these activities should serve not only to let people know about a show they might not be otherwise aware of, but also as a reminder to those who might mentally file and then forget an initial announcement of a show.

Beyond simply making people aware of the existence of a sponsored show, you can run promotions related to the show. A discount or premium could be offered to customers who say they saw a particular show or feature. For example, if a sporting goods store sponsors the weekly high school football coverage and names a "most valuable player" at the end of each broadcast, viewers coming into the store and identifying the most recent MVP would get a 10 percent discount coupon or a free keychain with a little football on the end of it.

CORPORATE COMMUNICATIONS

There is a subset of sponsored programming which is worth mentioning, and that is the use of cable as a means for companies to communicate with employees and/or stockholders. If a company has plants or offices in several areas, it can be economical to produce a cable program and distribute it to the cable systems serving the areas where employees can view it, rather than to print and mail pieces to a large number of individuals. Kaiser Aluminum and Chemical Company and Merck and Company are among the companies that have expanded their existing videotape employee communications programs by using cable in addition to internal distribution; one advantage of cable, officials of these companies have said, is that it lets employees' families and the general public also see the programs.

Several companies have produced video annual reports and purchased time to run them on cable networks or selected systems in order to address stockholders across the country. Anyone running a publicly held company knows that many of the stockholders receiving elaborate annual reports do not understand or even bother to read them. While every company has to abide by whatever SEC and/or other legal reporting requirements may apply to it, it might be possible in some cases to replace all or part of these printed reports with a cable program that can effectively inform stockholders. During the program the company can offer to mail financial statements to those who specifically request them through a toll-free telephone number or by mail. This type of approach could result in substantial cost savings over traditional reporting practices.

Note that for either of these types of programming to be effective, it is important to promote them adequately, just as one would a sponsored entertainment program. This is not that hard to do, especially in employee communications; a few interoffice memos sent to the various branches and plants and properly circulated can efficiently spread the word. Where more public notice is required, newspaper, program guide, radio, television, and cable ads can all be used as needed.

NINE

CABLE:
THE MULTIMEDIA MEDIUM

The relationship between cable systems and subscribers goes beyond providing video entertainment. It calls for communications on several other levels as well, from program guides that help the viewer choose among the many program offerings available to new technologies that permit the viewer to communicate with the cable system through the television set to the monthly cable service bill the viewer receives in the mail. Video, print, direct mail—each of these represents an opportunity for the advertiser to reach the cable subscriber, making cable the first truly multimedia medium.

I should make it quite clear before we continue that not every cable system offers all the services described in this chapter. Be sure to check first with any system you are interested in using.

PROGRAM GUIDES

One of the most common topics that comes up when people are discussing cable, both seriously and in jest, is just how they are going to decide what to watch when faced with a choice of 35, 50, 100 or more channels. One frequently heard comment is that once you've spent the time to push all the buttons to check out the channels, the program you've decided to watch is already over.

There are a number of sources from which subscribers can get information about cable programming, including television guides and newspaper television listings, but since these often cover areas served by more than one system, they tend not to be complete for any system. Even when there is no such conflict, some channels, particularly local origination and access channels, may not be included. As a result of the problems with these sources, many systems have arranged to offer subscribers customized, or "system-specific," cable program guides, tailored to their individual schedules. These usually are issued monthly, in magazine format, and consist of easily referenced comprehensive program listings combined with a variety of short articles relating to the monthly program offerings and other topics of interest. Often the publisher can add special features to the guide, such as wrappers and inserts; while these are generally provided for system promotional use, systems may make these options available to advertisers.

A few systems produce their guides in-house or locally, but many contract out to one of the dozen or so major guide publishers. The publisher produces a general magazine, usually in color, consisting of cable-related feature articles, which is wrapped around the individual system program listings section. This arrangement can be advantageous to national advertisers, since with one contract they can place an ad in the feature section of the guide which will then appear in all local editions of the guide. Ads can also be placed in the individual system listings; usually such sales orders are handled at the local level by the system or by the publisher.

Program guides are ideal for ensuring maximum subscriber coverage, since virtually every cable viewer who has not settled into an inflexible viewing routine will be consulting the guide throughout the entire month that it sits by the television, which means substantial frequency of exposure and cumulative effect. (By the way, if you think that ads in the listing sections are seen only on the days whose listings they appear adjacent to, try using a guide for a few days and see how many times you succeed in turning to the exact page you want when you pick it up and open it.)

In a study conducted for TVSM, a major guide publisher, in January 1983, Opinion Research Corporation uncovered some interesting statistics regarding program guide usage:

77 percent of single-pay homes and 82 percent of multi-pay homes look at the guide the day it arrives.

85 percent of cable subscribers use their guide at least once a day.

The typical single-pay cable subscriber uses the guide 2.3 times daily; the multi-pay subscriber, 2.7 times daily. Using that figure, together with A.C. Nielsen's estimate of 3.1 persons per average cable household, one program guide ad could generate over 200 exposures a month in a single household.

Ads in program guides can be self-standing, or you can tie them in with video ads or other related promotions. Coupons or similar redemption devices in these ads also help track the responsiveness of subscribers.

Another not-always-obvious benefit of program guides is that it lets advertisers who cannot use cable, such as liquor and cigarette companies, reach the upscale customers they do not otherwise have access to. However, some guides do have product category restrictions that should be checked. (More on the the issue of restricted advertisers in Chapter 14.)

Most systems that have the channel capacity to do so also offer some form of alphanumeric electronic program guide. Many of these are programmed by the systems, though several companies market a centrally produced custom service. These have several advantages over even the cable program guides. To paraphrase one company's slogan, the subscriber can't lose or throw away the electronic guide. It also tends to be more up-to-date than the paper guides, if for no other reason than that printed guides are published weeks in advance, whereas the electronic guide can be revised to reflect last-minute programming changes. According to an A.C. Nielsen study, 50 percent of cable viewers turn to the electronic guide 25 times a week, and 72 percent of those say the guide is very important in helping them choose and locate programs.

BILL STUFFERS

In recent years, you've undoubtedly noticed that it is not uncommon for your monthly credit card bills to include one or more extra pieces of paper, usually offering merchandise for sale, travel services, credit card protection services, and the like. In fact, at least one company mails its cardholders envelopes several times a year, each containing dozens of these little slips of paper, separate from the bills.

As another way of targeting the cable household, some cable systems allow advertisers to include similar pieces in their monthly subscriber bill mailings. Bill stuffers, as these inserts are often called, can serve several different purposes. They can be simply information sheets. They can be coupons redeemable by the subscriber for discounts or free goods. They can be miniature mail-order ads. They can stand on their own, or they can be crosspromotions with commercials being run on cable. Systems and networks use them regularly to promote programming or services.

When I profiled Albuquerque Cable Television (a Tribune Cable Communications system) in 1982, it reported great success with bill stuffer packages with both national and local advertisers. The system offered two packages: One included just the insert, which was mailed to those subscribers taking only the basic cable service; the other mailed the insert to all system subscribers, both basic-only and pay, and was tied to a 50-spot video commercial package. As it happened, when I contacted the system in 1983 to check on its success for inclusion in this book, I was advised that the bill stuffer program had been so successful for advertisers that the system's marketing department had taken all the available space for its own subscriber promotion activities. (The program has since been reopened to advertisers, with a greater variety of package options.)

Here are some guidelines to follow when using bill stuffers:

1.   Be sure to check with the cable system(s) you plan to use to see that they will in fact accept bill stuffers. There is concern in the cable industry that the privacy of subscribers not be compromised, so it is possible that systems will choose not to offer this option, even though the advertiser does not get direct access to the subscriber lists in these arrangements. On a more practical level, they just may not be equipped to handle bill stuffers. If a system has a relatively small billing operation (sometimes involving hand-stuffing bills in-house), it may not physically be able to incorporate additional items; likewise with larger and/or mech-

anized billing operations that have not set up facilities for handling inserts.

2.   Find out what the physical requirements are for inserts. Not only will there be the simple size specification (to fit them in the envelope), there may be certain requirements or restrictions that must be met where automatic stuffing equipment is used to handle the inserts. There may also be restrictions on the weight of the insert for postage or other reasons.

TEST MARKETING

The technological revolution has brought advances in many different areas, including test marketing. Testing has always been a major factor in introducing new products or campaigns, yet for all the many different testing techniques in existence, advertisers are still looking for ones that will allow greater control over all the variables that can affect the outcome of a test.

Cable is increasingly being utilized in test market situations. The low cost of cable advertising time makes test marketing much less expensive than using local television, while control over distribution of commercial messages by geographic area and programming makes it easier to keep tight control of test markets. Ironically, cable has even been used by at least one of the major television networks to test pilots for proposed series.

To some extent, cable can be used as a test marketing tool in connection with other technologies. For example, since cable lines reach specific homes, it is possible to make a controlled test of a product or commercial by introducing a spot on a local cable system and measuring the sales volume of the product at corresponding retail outlets using Universal Product Code (UPC) scanners, then measuring the results against outlets served by areas where the spot has not been run. Information Resources, Inc.'s BehaviorScan is a leading test service in this area. Since some cable systems have multiple distribution lines, you can even select specific segments within the system for coverage.

Advanced cable technology has been used to test commercials and to get consumer reaction to proposed products before they even go on the shelves. The Warner Amex cable system in Cincinnati, which is equipped with the company's QUBE interactive feature (which will be discussed further in Chapter 10), was the site for several such tests, these next two examples among them.

Licensing Corporation of America used the QUBE system to test consumer reaction to a variety of products it was considering licensing for manufacture. First, 30-second spots were run to invite people who met specified demographic characteristics and were willing to participate in a test that would be conducted over the cable system to so indicate by pushing a designated button on their QUBE control box. Those responding were later called by the cable system to confirm that they met the specifications. Prior to the test, verified respondents received reminders of the test date and a questionnaire to be returned after the test. The actual test was shown over one of the local origination channels, and the test audience was asked to rate on a 1 to 5 scale its liking (or dislike) of each product shown by pressing the appropriate QUBE button. (All subscribers who tuned into the channel could view the test, but only the preselected test viewers would have their responses counted by the computer.) During the test, the test viewers also filled in their questionnaires, explaining why they voted as they did on each product.

Investors Diversified Services, a financial services company, wanted to test a series of infomercials it had made for itself. It ran a show that began with a spokesman asking the viewers to watch the infomercials, which followed. After the last one had finished, the spokesman returned to poll the viewers on their opinions about the infomercials. At the end of the show, viewers could signal if they wanted to attend a free seminar conducted by IDS, have an IDS representative contact them, or receive a free brochure about IDS. (This test was also run on the Warner Amex system in Columbus, Ohio.)

PROMOTIONAL TIE-INS

Cable systems are very active themselves in advertising and promotion directed at the consumer to sell basic subscriptions and additional pay services. There may be local sales promotions by the cable system connected with its basic and/or pay cable services that would lend themselves to some form of sponsor activity. Often pay cable networks will run special campaigns in conjunction with local systems to try to sign up new subscribers, and may offer various types of premiums (mugs, tote bags, clothing, umbrellas) with the network's logo on them.[1] If a system wanted to conduct a campaign on its own, or otherwise wanted to offer premiums not available from the network, it might let an advertiser help underwrite (or contribute) premium items that could feature the advertiser's logo along with the network and/or system logos.

A variation on this theme is the situation where advertisers supply prizes for contests in return for mentions in the contest promotion and/or commercial tradeouts. In the summer of 1983 the Colony cable system in New Bedford and Fall River, Massachusetts, ran a $15,000 "Hot Time on Cable" sweepstakes. Although Colony underwrote the cash prizes itself, the car and travel prizes were obtained from local merchants through advertising tradeouts. Colony also sold advertising packages to a limited number of additional sponsors, which for $3,300 gave each one 150 30-second cable spots and free production of one 30-second commercial by the system, as well as substantial ancillary promotion. This included heavy promotion of the sweepstakes on the system and other area media (radio, newspapers, bus cards, in-store posters), and weekly highlighting of individual sponsors. Entry forms and boxes were placed in the sponsors' places of business. A number of sponsors, most of which were small retail outlets, said they saw many new faces come into their stores to fill out entry forms.

Some cable systems also offer nonprogramming services which, while not in and of themselves geared toward advertising, can offer promotion possibilities to the inventive advertiser. For example, in some systems, a home security system may be offered in connection with the cable hookup. These systems are tied in with

---

[1] While I am talking here about premiums given away by networks to encourage subscriber signups, note that premiums with joint network/advertiser identification have been quite popular as part of advertisers' own national or local efforts, such as an MTV/RC Cola bumper sticker giveaway run by an RC distributor in Illinois and a Nashville Network beverage cooler sold as a self-liquidating premium by Pepsi-Cola.

the cable and, should there be indication of a fire or break-in at the home, a signal is transmitted back down the line to the cable system headend, which can then notify the police or fire department. An advertiser might offer a booklet on home safety tips featuring its imprint, which could be given or mailed to subscribers when their security outlet is installed. (Alternatively, the booklet might be distributed by the cable system to all subscribers as part of a promotion to encourage new hookups for the security system.) An even simpler piece might be a sticker with various emergency service phone numbers printed on it (to be put on or near a phone).

TEN

DIRECT-RESPONSE ADVERTISING ON CABLE

Increases in transportation costs, demands on consumers' time brought about by more active lifestyles, and the growing number of working women are making direct purchasing more popular, as evidenced by the growth of mail-order and catalog sales. Direct marketers have found cable to be a very attractive medium because of the many advantages it offers them, and as a result direct response has become a major factor in cable advertising.

Direct response can be defined as an offering made in a commercial from which the viewer can order the product or service being advertised either by calling a toll-free number or writing to a particular address, usually a post office box.

The whole field of direct marketing has undergone a major change. Traditionally, in the minds of consumers and media people, television direct response meant cheap gadgets hawked by fast-talking announcers. Often they were marketed by less-than-reputable operators whose commitment to fulfilling orders was often less than total. This type of marginal operator has been virtually eliminated not only through the efforts of legitimate direct marketers, broadcasters, the Direct Marketing Association, and consumer protection legislation, but also through the sheer economics of the business. Above and beyond the actual cost of the product, the back end costs of marketing an item (the production and media charges for the commercial, processing and fulfilling orders, customer service, etc.) are setting higher price floors at which breakeven, much less a profit, can be achieved.

Consumers today, particularly those in cable's upscale households, are much more demanding and selective about what they purchase. Also, cable networks and systems have been setting higher standards for the types of offers for which they will accept advertising. As a result, the trend in direct marketing is toward higher-priced, better-quality, and more varied merchandise.

Naturally, the lower advertising cost of cable is attractive to direct marketers, who usually work with much smaller budgets than do major national advertisers. These initial cost savings clearly suggest that cable is an efficient buy, but efficiency also depends on the number of responses generated from a direct-marketing commercial and the cost of generating those responses. Does cable generate an adequate response for the money invested in it? Susan S. Aron of Saron Telecommunication Networks, Limited, addressed this question in a report she made to CAB on the marketing of a well-known product sold solely through direct-response television and cable.

The advertiser spent $865,250 to buy 1,031 60-second spots on a combination of independent and local network affiliate television stations and received 25,000 responses. The same advertiser also received 25,000 responses from an investment of $600,000 in 706 60-second spots on a combination of network and local cable. This comes out to 24.2 responses per spot produced by broadcast television at a cost of $34.77 per response, as opposed to 35.4 responses per spot produced by cable television at a cost of $24 per response.

The overall cost difference of $269,250 can be utilized to buy 317 additional spots on cable that would result in 11,224 additional responses, for a total of 36,224 responses produced by cable television for the same amount of money that brought in 25,000 responses through broadcast television.

Explaining that she had found this same pattern in similar situations, Ms. Aron concluded:

> The benefits to a direct-response advertiser are clear, and
> are translatable to all advertisers since the overall objectives
> of advertising include generating response that will result

TO GENERATE 25,000 RESPONSES

MEDIUM	SPOTS BOUGHT	COST	TOTAL RESPONSES	RESPONSES PER SPOT	COST PER RESPONSE
Broadcast	1,031	$869,250	25,000	24.2	$34.77
Cable	706	600,000	25,000	35.4	24.00

TO PLACE $869,250 IN SPOT BUYS

MEDIUM	SPOTS BOUGHT	COST	TOTAL RESPONSES	RESPONSES PER SPOT	COST PER RESPONSE
Broadcast	1,031	$869,250	25,000	24.2	$34.77
Cable	1,023	869,250	36,224	35.4	24.00

Data shown projected from actual response.

SOURCE: Saron Telecommunication Networks, Limited.

in sales or opinion change. Since cable television stimulates and activates its viewers in greater proportions for less money than broadcast television, its value to an advertiser increases with every additional subscriber. The effectiveness of the medium increases with every additional system and network utilized to reach defined target audiences.

In this example, the advertiser bought broadcast and cable on a cash basis, the way most regular advertising is purchased. A large amount of direct-response activity, though, is done on what is known as a *per-inquiry* basis. With per-inquiry, the network or system is not paid for the media time used, but instead receives a commission based on the number of responses generated by the commercial. Where merchandise is being sold, this will usually be a portion of the sales price (say, $3 on a $14.95 item); if the offer is for a free item, such as an information booklet about a service, a negotiated amount will be paid by the advertiser for each request received.

GUIDELINES FOR ADVERTISERS

I asked the direct-response specialists at several cable networks, direct marketing firms, and the Direct Marketing Association what advice or guidelines they would offer advertisers looking to use direct response on cable. Here is a summary of their comments and suggestions.

• *Four criteria for success.*   Although there are no magic formulas that can guarantee a successful direct-response offering, there are four criteria which, if met, may improve a product's chances for success:

1. The product should be unique. While it is certainly possible to sell commonly available items through direct response, most of the major direct-marketing successes have been with products different from those already on the market. Products can be completely new, or significant variations on existing items. In any event, they should be perceived as worth the money not only in the commercial, but when the buyer opens the box and uses them.

2. The product should be perceived as meeting the customer's needs or interests, whether useful, instructional, or recreational. The customer must be sufficiently attracted to the product not only to want to purchase it, but to be willing to wait for the several weeks it may take to arrive and, if COD, to accept delivery when it does.

3. The product should not be available locally. If the consumer is sufficiently motivated to buy the product, he or she may prefer to buy it immediately at the local department store rather than wait for it to be delivered from the direct marketer. Retail sales, though, may be a good aftermarket once direct sales have run their course (in-store merchandise packages can then be labeled "as advertised on cable").

4. The product should be demonstrable. It is much harder, even in the usually extended time of a direct-response commercial, to sell a product the viewer cannot see in use.

In situations where the first four criteria are not met, familiar merchandise can be offered at a significant price savings over the regular price and/or those of competing products. (A good example is discounted magazine subscriptions, which are among the most popular direct-response offers on cable.)

• *The proper expertise.*   Advertisers not experienced in direct marketing should enlist the services of a direct marketing company or advertising agency specializing in the field. The days when a lone inventor could manufacture and market a product out of a garage are pretty much past, as the intricacies of effective direct marketing today are many and require special expertise.

A good direct-marketing operation will evaluate your product's sales potential, perhaps suggest modifications that will make it more salable, oversee the production of a suitable commercial, test your product, and design and place the commercial schedule. It may also handle or else make provision for a fulfillment house to process the orders. (In some cases, cable networks themselves have made arrangements for a telephone marketing company to take all the orders for all their direct-response clients not so equipped.) The Direct Marketing Association can help you locate a suitable firm; many direct advertising agencies can also be found by using the Special Market Index in the *Standard Directory of Advertising Agencies* (The Red Book), published quarterly by National Register Publishing Company.

• *Effective commercials.*   Direct-response commercials should be well-produced, informative, and to the point. Two minutes has proved to be an effective length for direct-response commercials, as it allows enough time to demonstrate and sell the product and still leave room for the tag. Since most people do not watch cable with a phone or notepad at their elbow, the tag should be on the screen for 20 to 30 seconds in order to give the viewer a chance to find pencil and paper and copy down the address and/or phone number. Superimposing the phone number over part or all of the sales message as well as the tag has increased response rates as much as 100 percent on some commercials.

In the tag, the phone number and/or address should be repeated verbally several times while it is being shown on the screen, so that it penetrates the viewer's mind and is more easily remembered until it is written down. Numbers are easier to recall or capture if they have some kind of "rhythm" or sequence to them. For example, 555-1234 and 222-5000 are much easier to remember than 617-4925 or 415-3081; similarly, P.O. Box 777 is better than P.O. Box 32614. While your choices may be limited by what the telephone companies and post offices you use have available, it is worth the extra effort to try to find easy-to-remember phone and box numbers.

With the increased use of toll-free 800 numbers has come a tendency to try to make them easier to remember by using words and letter/number combinations as mnemonic devices. It may in fact be better to avoid this practice, since some phones now being manufactured have only numbers on their buttons or dials. Numbers like 321-ROCK, USA-1984, or BIG-DEAL are great for memory, but a problem when the would-be caller can't remember or find out their numerical equivalents on the dial. Using different numbered phones or boxes can be very helpful in per-inquiry advertising for identifying where the orders are coming from and checking cost per order by network or system; don't expect the viewer to be able to tell you where he or she saw your commercial, particularly if he or she doesn't call the moment after it runs.

It is often advisable to produce 60- and/or 90-second commercials in addition to a 2-minute version. Two-minute spot blocks may not always be available, and having different-length spots allows for more flexibility in scheduling. While the shorter spots may not be as effective as a 2-minute one, being able to clear a wider schedule and build frequency can even out the response rate per dollar invested.

• Payment options.   One telephone marketer cited in a Direct Marketing Association report suggested offering a COD purchase option as well as credit card phone orders in order to increase response rates. Another pointed out, though, that many people will order only by COD, even if you specifically say "No CODs" in the commercial.

However, both networks and marketers said they have found that a much higher percentage of respondents to the commercials run on cable use credit cards or prepayment, and that the number of COD refusals is much lower than occurs with sales from broadcast television.

Even so, some network people suggested that the COD option not be offered when placing advertising in programming or dayparts likely to have minors viewing. This can help avoid the problem of parents refusing to accept or pay for merchandise ordered by their children without their knowledge and/or approval.

• Prompt order fulfillment.   Every marketer I spoke to noted the importance of having adequate and efficient order acceptance and fulfillment capabilities, whether they are in-house

or contracted out to a specialist. With the proliferation of credit card usage and CODs, orders can and should be filled promptly. The customer's wait of "4 to 6 weeks for delivery," which was designed to make sure that checks cleared the bank before merchandise was shipped, can now be reduced substantially.

It is very important to have enough product on hand and available for prompt order fulfillment. Do *not* wait until after orders have started to pile up to manufacture the product to fit the demand. Several network people said that they expect to be shown a warehouse full of the merchandise to be advertised before they will run a direct-response commercial. According to the marketers, though, what is needed is enough inventory to handle all orders received during the periods between the manufacturer's shipments to the fulfillment center. The real problem, one added, occurs when the manufacturer can produce 4,000 units a week and orders start coming in at the rate of 12,000 a week; in that case, arrangements should be made to contract out production while coordinating quality control and shipping in order to have orders filled on a timely basis.

• *Customer service.*   Irwin Barnett, one of the country's leading direct-response consultants, repeatedly emphasized the need for good customer service, including unconditionally guaranteeing what you sell and letting the buyer know that you do so. If the customer complains about the product and wants a refund, says Mr. Barnett, you should send it out promptly, no questions asked.

This isn't a question of altruism, he added, but of business economics. Except with very expensive items, it is far cheaper for an advertiser to refund the purchase price than to spend the time fighting with or ignoring the disgruntled customer, especially if the latter course may result in any form of legal action or inquiry (even a 15-minute phone call to a lawyer for advice on answering a lawsuit threat could cost more than the refund on a $29.95 item). On top of that, there is the cost of the time the company might have to spend dealing with consumer protection agencies or activists. Prompt resolution of a complaint can save a lot of time, money, and hassle, and at the same time garner goodwill with the customer, who may then still consider buying from you in the future.

Perhaps more to the point, when customers are unhappy with something they have purchased from a direct-response commercial, they don't always write to the marketer to complain; they often write to the head of the cable network or system that carried the commercial. Network presidents and system managers do not like getting these kinds of letters, and they will expect you to handle any complaints promptly. It does not take many such letters before they may refuse to let you advertise with them.

Most networks and systems screen direct-response clients carefully before they will accept their advertising. I mentioned earlier that they check that inventory is available for shipping. They may also check credit references, payment record, and track record of the client; the quality of the product and the legitimacy of any claims made for it; and/or the compatibility of the product and the commercial with their own image and offerings. For per-inquiry buys, they will want to evaluate the efficiency of the offering in terms of its expected response levels and return to them, since as a de facto partner in the offering they will want to accept only items that will give them the maximum return for the cablecast time used. It is not uncommon for a cash advance to be required from PI advertisers.

One advertiser that found success in direct response on cable was, interestingly enough, the Direct Marketing Association itself. To promote its *Great Catalogue Guide,* a catalog of over 600 mail-order catalogs of all kinds, as well as to test the efficiency of cable as a direct marketing medium, the DMA ran a schedule of two-minute commercials on the SPN and ESPN cable networks over a two-week period. In this well-made commercial, created by the Grey Direct agency, viewers were shown the wide variety of items available by mail order and given an 800 number to call to get the free *Great Catalogue Guide.* Expectations were that around 2,000 responses might be received; in actuality, *over 7,000* requests were phoned in by viewers.

King Size, a mail-order firm that specializes in clothing for large-size men, used ESPN as the vehicle for promoting its catalog. A commercial offering the free catalog via an 800 number was run 20 times a week over a three-week period, with responses exceeding 400 requests each day.

Fifty copies of a limited edition Leroy Neiman serigraph priced at $1,250 each were sold during a six-week ROS run on ESPN. A Norman Rockwell painting was auctioned over the same network. With the minimum price set at $120,000 and only one spot run each night over a three-week period, 60 responses were received, and the painting was finally sold for $135,000.

One might think that ESPN viewers would be quick to snap up any kind of sports-related merchandise, but this isn't always the case. Many tennis and golf accessories have been advertised with little or no success. Then one day an advertiser came in wanting to sell a line of golf shoes. The network sales people were a bit dubious, given the track record to date of golf aids, and the difficulty of selling any item that has to be sized to fit the customer. During the summer the commercials ran, 250 pairs of shoes were sold each week. Subsequently the same advertiser marketed a golf putter that sold 150 units a week.

Then there was the person who wanted to sell a new product which he claimed would, when applied to fish bait, attract more fish. A relatively low-key commercial for the product featured a well-known sports fisherman as the spokesman. He suggested no more than that the product *might* help other fishermen increase their catches. The first day the spot aired, 1,000 bottles were sold, and a year later orders were still being received at the rate of 1,000 a month.

As I mentioned earlier, periodicals seem to be a universal success on cable. Most networks report success with them, as do their agencies. Sheldon Hechtman of Rapp & Collins said: "Time and time again, cable has proven to be a hell of a lot stronger than over-the-air television [for selling specialized magazines]. I've had magazines that I couldn't sell on broadcast that have done very well on cable."

One of the great direct-response successes of recent years has been the Bamboo Steamer, with 3.7 million units sold in the first three years. Frank Brady, chairman of Urban General Corporation, which marketed the product, estimated that some 60 percent of those sales came from cable viewers. Other Urban General offerings have generated sales of as much as 10,000 units a week.

INTERACTIVE CABLE

One of the popular buzzwords in cable is "interactive" or "two-way" cable. Basically this refers to cable systems that have the technical ability to let subscribers communicate directly with a computer at the system headend from their television sets, using special converters and the same cable lines that bring them their programming. So far, relatively few systems have offered this type of service, mostly due to the high equipment costs involved. In anticipation of future installation, though, since the mid-1970s many systems have been built with coaxial cable capable of handling the service.

Warner Amex Cable Communications has been a leader in this area, with several of its systems offering subscribers the company's QUBE interactive service.[1] Using the same hand-held box that serves as a remote-control channel selector, QUBE viewers are able to respond to multiple-choice questions posed on the screen. In most situations the QUBE feature is used for taking informal, nonscientific polls of viewer opinions, with the response figures displayed on the screen (in percentages) within seconds. This feature has become so popular that it has been used to take viewer polls from the Warner Amex system in Columbus, Ohio, on live national programming such as CNN's *Take Two* news program and the short-lived NBC program, *Speak Up, America*.

While ordinary viewer polling is handled on an anonymous and aggregate basis, the fact is that the computer which tabulates viewer votes is also capable of identifying the household from which a response signal is coming, much the way telephone company computers can identify when any particular phone is in use. The cable system uses this feature in connection with security and fire alarm systems connected to the cable, and also for offering pay-per-view programming (special one-time programs for which viewers pay an extra fee should they order them). This same feature has been successfully used for advertising-related situations as well.[2]

---

[1] I should probably take a moment to mention here that, as a result of the publicity surrounding the Warner Amex installations, many people use the term QUBE to describe any two-way cable system. In fact, QUBE is a trademark that refers only to Warner Amex interactive systems and any others specifically licensed to use the name. The hardware used in QUBE systems is also used in other cable systems under other names, and there are several other interactive hardware systems from different manufacturers in use around the country.

[2] Some difficulties can arise with interactive cable advertising, particularly when viewers are requesting that they be sent something or contacted by the advertiser. The issues regarding privacy laws and information gathered by two-way cable technology are quite complex. Warner Amex developed and adopted its

In terms of direct response, the viewer interested in purchasing a product being advertised no longer has to be concerned with scrambling for pencil and paper to copy an address or telephone number from a commercial, nor with remembering to place an order by mail or phone. All the person has to do is to push the appropriate button at the right time, and the cable system computer will supply the advertiser with the customer's name and address for order processing. Here are a few examples of how interactive cable has been used for advertising purposes in the Warner Amex QUBE systems in Ohio.

American Express Travel Services ran a series of infomercials showing how to pick a travel agent, understand tour brochures, and generally make all the decisions involved in planning a vacation. At the end of the program, viewers who were interested in receiving information on American Express tours could press a response button on their control box. Within the next 48 hours, the system would send the requested brochures with a cover letter from the local American Express travel agent thanking the respondent for his or her interest. Respondents subsequently received invitations to attend special screenings of a half-hour film on American Express vacations, and followup phone calls offering additional information after that. All of this was very information-oriented and soft-sell, yet resulted in the lowest cost per sale for any American Express travel agent in the country.

Another venture with American Express was run in Cincinnati. This time it was in conjunction with the credit card division. The system created a series called *Eating Out in Cincinnati* in which viewers were introduced to some of the better restaurants in the area. In each segment, the host gave a tour of the particular establishment being featured, then the chef would demonstrate the preparation of a dish the restaurant was noted for. At the end of the

---

own Code of Privacy in 1982 in order to protect its subscribers' interests. Its operative rules include informing viewers in advance whenever their responses will not be anonymous and strictly controlling the handling of those responses. Wherever the viewer requests that something be sent to him or her, Warner Amex handles the mailings; the advertiser receives only a response count, no names or addresses. In cases where the viewer asks that he or she be contacted by the advertiser, Warner Amex does supply names and addresses, but only after the advertiser has signed a stringent contract limiting use of those data only to answering those requests.

demonstration, viewers could touch in if they wanted to receive a copy of the recipe. Those viewers would be sent the recipes on cards that featured the recipe on one side and the American Express card logo on the reverse.

Warner Cosmetics has used the QUBE systems in Cincinnati, Columbus, Dallas, and Pittsburgh to promote the Ralph Lauren cosmetics line on several occasions. In December 1982 the first co-op effort for the line on QUBE was made in association with Lazarus, the Federated Department Stores branch in Columbus. In this test, a 30-minute program demonstrating makeup techniques for daytime and nighttime looks for the holidays was produced at the QUBE system and shown twice a day over a two-week period. Viewers were invited to touch in on their control boxes if they wanted to get a free Ralph Lauren makeover, and 1,682 out of the 11,600 who tuned in responded. When called by the store, 800 of these respondents actually set up appointments for their makeovers; 48 percent showed up for their appointments, which was a greater response rate than had been realized with any other medium. Not only that, those people who received makeovers made purchases averaging over $50 each, which gave the store an additional $20,000 revenue during what is usually a very slow time for cosmetics sales.

In April 1984 another 30-minute interactive program, *Spring Looks from Ralph Lauren Cosmetics,* was presented on the QUBE-equipped systems in the four cities listed above, again in association with the Federated Department Store in each city.

Avon cosmetics appeared on the Columbus system in a series of three company-sponsored shows hosted by Julia Meade. Through the QUBE feature, viewers were able to choose the subject of the next show in the series, purchase sweatsuits, and even express interest in becoming an Avon sales representative.

In Cincinnati, Merrill Lynch used the QUBE system to introduce high-yield investments to viewers. Merrill Lynch had previously conducted by closed-circuit satellite a seminar on these types of investments for large-volume customers around the country. The system took a tape that had been made of the seminar and ran it several times during a one-week period. Each showing was tagged with a promotional message that invited viewers to tune in at the end of the week for a live call-in program with local Merrill Lynch executives in which they could have any questions answered. During the call-in show, the QUBE feature was used to get input from viewers and, at the end, to offer them the opportunity to request that Merrill Lynch contact them directly.

Interactive cable can also be used to supplement existing advertising running on cable or broadcast television. In Columbus, the Warner Amex system inserted interactive overlays on top of Kraft commercials in a CBS television special carried by the local CBS affiliate station. While the television commercials told viewers they could find a set of recipes published in that week's issue of *TV Guide*, QUBE subscribers could use their control boxes to request that those recipes be sent to them directly. (The overlays consisted of a one-line alphanumeric crawl run across the bottom of the screen during the commercials. Since they did not preempt or interfere with the regular television image and they were done at Kraft's request with the consent of the TV station, there was no conflict with the noninterruption rule mentioned in footnote 1 on page 39.)

Although the expense of the hardware for and maintenance of interactive cable has limited its installation to only a handful of systems around the country to date, interactivity can be a valuable direct-marketing tool in those areas where it is available. It may expand should the cable industry become further involved in computer-based services that can use home computers instead of separate control boxes as response terminals. With such systems, viewers could not only order an item they see offered, but also access detailed information about the item, select sizes/colors/other specifications, and have payment made automatically by credit card or bank transfer.

ELEVEN

CO-OP ADVERTISING ON CABLE

If you're a retailer, you may not be getting all that you should out of your advertising budget. For years, many manufacturers have helped cover their retailers' advertising costs through cooperative advertising programs, usually known as co-op. Now, largely through the joint efforts of CAB and the Co-op Committee of the Association of National Advertisers, information about the availability of co-op funds for cable has become more widespread. CAB's own co-op service is helping cable systems keep up to date on many cable co-op plans and enabling them to help retailers take advantage of those plans, as well as encouraging manufacturers to include cable in their co-op plans.

Cable co-op offers significant advantages to the retailer. It expands advertising budgets and allows increases in the number and/or length of commercials as well as the variety of products featured. It also helps put the retailer in a better competitive position with other merchants selling the same or similar goods. Very often it enables a retailer to run local advertisements in conjunction with a national or regional campaign being run by the manufacturer, with the tie-in proving advantageous to both parties by improving the retailer's image and encouraging additional sales.

It is relatively simple to find out what co-op funds are available from manufacturers. By law, manufacturers are required to inform all their retailers of their co-op programs. Usually they will place announcements of the programs in the appropriate trade journals and/or send copies of the plans directly to the retailers; often the manufacturer's sales representatives will also personally discuss the co-op plans with the retailers they call on. Several companies publish directories of manufacturer's co-op advertising plans, such as Standard Rate and Data Service's *Co-op Source Directory* or BMC's *Co-opportunities* service.

While co-op is not really all that complicated, it does require a little extra effort to develop. For one thing, there are several terms and procedures that you don't have with other advertising and that often require additional paperwork. Since co-op plan information can come in a variety of formats, it may be a little hard to decipher at first. These are the main items you should be looking for when reading a co-op plan:

• *Name and address of company, contact person and telephone number.*   This is important because in some instances the company offering the co-op plan may not be the actual manufacturer of the items in question; it could be a distributor or agent. The contact is the person you should get in touch with if you have questions or problems.

• *Products and brands/trademarks.*   Co-op plans always indicate exactly which of the company's products and specific brands thereof are eligible for co-op dollars. *Do not assume that products not listed are also covered.* If you do not see a particular product or brand you are interested in listed, check with the manufacturer's co-op contact person to see if it is covered by a different plan.

• *Accrual.*   This refers to the amount of co-op dollars earned by the retailer. In most cases it is a percentage (as a rule, 1 to 10 percent) of the value of the retailer's purchases of the eligible products during a given period. It may also be a flat amount per quantity purchased or per retailer, and there may be maximum or minimum limits on the amounts accruable.

Manufacturers are required, in addition to keeping retailers informed of their co-op plans, to be able to advise each retailer upon request of the dollar amount of co-op funds it has accrued.

Naturally, larger retailers who purchase more of the manufacturer's product will accrue more funds than will smaller customers; however, manufacturers must offer access to their co-op funds to *all* retailers in the market(s) in which the plan is being offered. (They are not required, though, to offer co-op plans in all markets, and you should always check plans to see if there are any market variations or restrictions that may affect you.)

• *Timing.*   There are three major time elements to be dealt with in co-op. The first is the *accrual period;* this is the period during which retailer purchases earn co-op funds. The second is the *advertising period,* during which the retailer's advertising must appear in order to qualify for co-op reimbursement. The third is the *claim period,* during which any claims for reimbursement must be submitted, usually within 30 to 90 days of the ad run. *Co-op funds not utilized within the designated co-op period are forfeited.*

• *Participation or allowance.*   The share of the advertising costs the manufacturer will pay for is often expressed as a percentage ratio. A 75-25 plan is one where the manufacturer pays 75 percent of the advertising costs (up to the total accrual amount earned) and the retailer pays the other 25 percent. The manufacturer may also indicate what costs it will or will not help pay for, such as commercial production charges, agency fees, or media charges.

• *Eligible media and media requirements.*   Not all plans can be used in all media. Each plan should indicate which types of advertising are eligible for co-op reimbursement. Often the manufacturer will indicate specific requirements for eligible media; more often than not, prior approval to use cable must be obtained from the manufacturer.

If there is any question as to whether cable is eligible for co-op, or if you have any other questions regarding the existence or terms of a co-op program or the amount of funds you have accrued, the best thing to do is to write directly to the manufacturer's co-op advertising manager. Since that person is required to keep retailers informed about co-op, you should receive a prompt reply. Here is a sample letter you can use when writing to manufacturers:

> Dear *Co-op Advertising Manager:*
> We are interested in setting up a cable television advertising program for *product(s)* with *name of cable*

system. Please send us information on how to implement this.

We need a copy of your current co-op plan as soon as possible, together with information on the amount of co-op funds we have accrued to date so that we can plan a cable schedule that meets your requirements.

We look forward to receiving this information.

If you also want information about commercials or copy available, you may want to add the following paragraph to your letter:

As we wish to be certain we meet your copy requirements, please advise us as to how to obtain any commercials, scripts, or production elements that would be available to us to use in our cable advertising campaign. If no such materials are available, please let us know as soon as possible so that we can promptly arrange to produce a commercial that will meet with your approval.

At some point you may want to involve the cable system in your communications with the manufacturer, particularly if you intend to create your own commercial or to adapt creative material supplied with the manufacturer's plan.

• Advertising requirements. As noted above, the manufacturer will often have certain copy or other specifications that must be met in retailer ads in order to qualify for co-op reimbursement. In cable, the concern is usually the amount of time the manufacturer's product appears on screen and/or is mentioned in the audio portion of the commercial. To help meet these requirements, manufacturers may have production material available for retailers' use. These could be fully produced commercials for particular products that need nothing more than the dealer tag added, or they could be shorter production elements than can be edited into a retailer's own spot. Even if such tape or film pieces are not available, artwork supplied by the manufacturer for print media use can often be used in creating cable spots (see page 62).

• Claim documentation. Manufacturers, of course, require documentation of advertising in order to effect reim-

bursement. Each manufacturer will specify what proof of performance is required under each co-op plan, but as a rule standard documentation will include an invoice or other proof of rates charged for the spots run and an affidavit from the cable system showing how many spots ran and when. Other materials that may be requested include commercial scripts and manufacturer's claim forms.

In 1981, in order to help standardize and simplify documentation procedures for cable co-op, the Association of National Advertisers and the Cabletelevision Advertising Bureau jointly developed the ANA/CAB Cabletelevision Co-op Documentation Form. The form follows existing broadcast media co-op procedures which the ANA helped to establish in years past. When completed by the cable system, the form contains: (a) the name and address of the system, the retailer that placed the ads, and the manufacturer being billed for co-op reimbursement; (b) the script(s) of the spot(s) used (or transcriptions of manufacturers' videotapes if used); and (c) an affidavit by the system indicating the number of spots run, the rate for those spots, and the total cost. A system official must sign the form and, if required, have it notarized. A receipted invoice is then attached to the documentation form.

Manufacturers will usually require that documentation be returned directly to their offices. Often, though, a co-op plan will indicate that documentation is to be sent to the Advertising Checking Bureau (ACB). ACB is a company that audits co-op activity for sponsoring manufacturers, verifying that claims are properly documented, complete, and accurate. Once it has reviewed a claim and found the documentation satisfactory, it will approve reimbursement. Pinpoint Marketing Inc. is another widely used company providing similar services.

Sometimes retailers find that they do not make enough purchases of a particular item to generate a significant amount of co-op dollars, and so do not bother to do anything with them. This violates one of Barr's Laws of Money, namely: "Every little bit helps." If you find yourself in this position, there are still things you can do to make use of these funds. First, see if the manufacturer has different co-op plans under which you earn accruals; there may be enough combined funds available to allow you to run a series of commercials featuring different products in different spots. You might also check with the manufacturer to see if it will allow you

> Use your system copy paper or following suggested letterhead.
> Statement at bottom must be exactly as shown.

ANA/CAB CABLETELEVISION CO-OP DOCUMENTATION FORM

_____

_____

_____

(SYSTEM /ADDRESS / MARKET)

Client: _____   Manufacturer: _____

_____   _____

_____   _____

Begin: _____   End: _____   Date: _____

SCRIPT

➤ Stamp or print this form on bottom of your script paper

**DOCUMENTATION STATEMENT APPROVED BY THE CO-OPERATIVE ADVERTISING COMMITTEE OF
THE ASSOCIATION OF NATIONAL ADVERTISERS AND THE CABLETELEVISION ADVERTISING BUREAU.**

This announcement was cablecast _____ times, as entered in the system's program log. The times this announcement
was cablecast were billed to this system's client on our invoice(s) numbered /dated _____ at his earned rate of:

$ _____ each for _____ announcements, for a total of $ _____

$ _____ each for _____ announcements, for a total of $ _____

$ _____ each for _____ announcements, for a total of $ _____

Sworn to and subscribed before me and in my
presence on this _____ day of _____ . 19 _____

_____

Signature of system official

(Notarize above)   **Typed name and title**   **System**

to run spots featuring more than one product and receive pro rata reimbursement from the respective plans.

Another way to extend the impact of smaller accruals is the use of multiproduct ads featuring different manufacturers. This can raise problems because most manufacturers want their names and products given prominence in commercials they co-op. Care must be taken that commercials meet these requirements, especially those featuring more than one manufacturer or brand.

Another common solution is to try to combine not products, but retailers. Under this approach, a manufacturer or distributor will bring several dealers together to form what is known as a dealer group, which pools the accrued co-op earnings of each dealer into a joint fund that pays for ads sponsored by the group. You have undoubtedly seen these used in television commercials that are tagged either for the group as a whole ("See your local tri-state Widget dealer") or for each retailer (or several at a time, depending on the time available and tag method used) on a rotating basis.

Many retailers are often surprised by the number of co-op plans available to them. Once you begin drawing on these funds, you will find it valuable to set up files to keep track of available plans so as to be able to take full advantage of your accrual potential. There are several ways you can go about this. One is to keep the plans on file by manufacturer, product type, or other product identification you find easy to work with. In combination with this, you should set up a calendar with which you can easily track the accrual and advertising periods for each plan; this will let you plan your purchasing and advertising of eligible merchandise in the most effective way.

Here's one example of how co-op can work for a retailer: Jones Appliance is a medium-size dealer in Midville. Among the products Rick Jones sells are Kleanmore washing machines. After a talk with Susan Smith, the advertising salesperson from the local cable system, he finds out that Kleanmore is offering the following co-op plan:

KLEANMORE INCORPORATED
One Washington Avenue
Bigapple, USA 99999
(909) 555-4000

Contact: John Brown, Co-op Advertising Manager
Product/Brands: Kleanmore washers and dryers
Accruals: 5% of net purchases, January 1–June 30, 19X5
Participation: 50–50, for time charges only. Ads must run between July 1 and December 31, 19X5.
Eligible media: Television and cable. Prior approval required.
Advertising specifications: Product(s) must be illustrated. Manufacturer's logo required. No competing products. Minimum of 50% of commercial must be devoted to manufacturer's products.
Advertising aids: Television production elements available.
Claim documentation: ANA/TvB co-op documentation form (ANA/CAB form for cable), script, media invoice. Submit claims to manufacturer within 60 days following run of commercial.

It is now August 1, 19X5, and Jones is planning his Columbus Day sale. He knows that he purchased $10,000 worth of Kleanmore washers and dryers in the first six months of the year, so he figures he has accrued $500 (5 percent × $10,000) in co-op credit from Kleanmore. He calls John Brown to verify the accrual, to inquire about approval for using cable, and to request a copy of the production elements. Brown verifies the accrual, says that he can approve cable once Jones can give him an idea of how many spots will be run and when, and adds that he will have the production tape, which contains excerpts from Kleanmore's national television commercials, sent to Susan Smith right away.

Jones calls Smith; they meet and work out a schedule of 25 prime time spots at $40 each. Smith has received the tape from Kleanmore and prepared a commercial script for Jones Appliance featuring the Kleanmore products; she adds that it will cost $100 to tape the new material for the commercial and edit it. After making some minor changes, Jones approves the spot; at his request, Smith sends a copy of the spot schedule and the script to Brown, who notifies Jones that the campaign has been approved for co-op reimbursement.

The cable system's production staff produces the Jones Appliance commercial, and it is run once each weeknight for five weeks beginning in September. Each week the system has supplied

Jones with documentation for the previous week's commercials, which Jones reviews before submitting the entire package to Brown.

With the co-op reimbursement from Kleanmore, Jones's costs look like this:

Week	Spots	Rate	Total	Jones Pays	Kleanmore Pays	Co-op $ Available
0						$500
1	5	$40	$ 200	$100	$100	400
2	5	40	200	100	100	300
3	5	40	200	100	100	200
4	5	40	200	100	100	100
5	5	40	200	100	100	-0-
Total	25		$1,000	$500	$500	

Instead of paying $1,000 for this campaign, Jones has spent only $500 (not counting the commercial production costs, which he would have incurred anyway, since they were not covered by co-op; the use of Kleanmore's production elements, though, may have resulted in some savings here). He has saved $500 which he now can use to purchase additional advertising at regular rates or for whatever other purpose he chooses.

In this example, the situation was designed so that the co-op dollars and the advertising costs would come out evenly. It doesn't always work out quite this neatly; here's what else can happen. Let's assume that Jones decided to run a six-week campaign with the same parameters rather than a five-week one. His time costs would be as shown on p. 108.

Jones has used up his co-op allowance after the fifth week, so any additional costs he has to pay himself. There is certainly nothing wrong with this, and there is no reason why you should allow your co-op allowances to limit your advertising. Co-op should be looked upon as an aid, not a restriction. In this case, Jones has still realized a $500 savings, regardless of how much additional advertising he chooses to place.

The problem with co-op comes when you don't use it efficiently. Let us assume that Jones, for whatever reason, is either

Week	Spots	Rate	Total	Jones Pays	Kleanmore Pays	Co-op $ Available
0						$500
1	5	$40	$ 200	$100	$100	400
2	5	40	200	100	100	300
3	5	40	200	100	100	200
4	5	40	200	100	100	100
5	5	40	200	100	100	-0-
6	5	40	200	200	-0-	-0-
Total	30		$1,200	$700	$500	

unaware of or does not choose to use his accrued co-op funds until November, when he decides to run a four-week campaign between Thanksgiving and Christmas (again, with the same parameters):

Week	Spots	Rate	Total	Jones Pays	Kleanmore Pays	Co-op $ Available
0						$500
1	5	$40	$200	$100	$100	400
2	5	40	200	100	100	300
3	5	40	200	100	100	200
4	5	40	200	100	100	100
Total	20		$800	$400	$400	

Jones doesn't run any advertising after Christmas, nor does he run any additional spots during the four weeks of his campaign. As a result, he forfeits the $100 remaining in his accrual account, since the plan required that it be used before December 31. With that $100 allowance, he could have had up to five additional spots half paid for by Kleanmore, which could have let him run spots on weekends or extra spots during that last critical week before Christmas.

While Jones has found a means to use co-op effectively, some of the smaller appliance dealers in Average County who sell Kleanmore products have not been able to do so because they do not purchase enough inventory to earn significant allowances. They have decided it would be to everyone's benefit to form a countywide dealer group in order to pool co-op resources, and have asked Acme, the Kleanmore distributor serving the county, to help put the group together. Fortunately all twelve dealers agree, and the Average County Kleanmore "Klean Team" is established.

The following July, Acme checks its sales records and finds that the twelve stores have collectively purchased $80,000 worth of Kleanmore products during the January–June accrual period, entitling the group to a $4,000 co-op allowance. Since the cable systems serving Average County are interconnected, and the prime time spot rate for the interconnect is $100, the "Klean Team" can purchase 80 prime time spots countywide. The decision is made to run one spot every weeknight over the 16 weeks between Labor Day and Christmas. The Midville cable system produces a commercial which, besides advertising the Kleanmore line, invites viewers to "Clean Up With the Klean Team" and lists three of the dealers at the end. Producing the commercial costs $150 (the extra cost comes from making four different dubs in order to get all twelve dealers included in the tags),[1] but even if they decide to produce five more spots to adjust for the changing months and holiday sales, the total production cost to each dealer still would average out to $75 for all six spots.

Of course, the dealers could just as easily decide not to spread themselves over a long period, but rather concentrate their effort by using more spots over a shorter time period, particularly if either they or Kleanmore run any kind of major sales promotion somewhere along the line.

It is important to understand that throughout these examples, I have discussed co-op from only one manufacturer. Actually, a store such as Jones Appliance would undoubtedly carry the products of many manufacturers and would have many co-op plans available to it. Multiply Jones's experience by, say, 20 brands, and you see the amount of advertising power co-op can give him.[2]

---

[1] Actually, the number of tag appearances for each dealer would usually be determined by the each dealer's individual accrual taken as a proportion of the group's total allowance, rather than evenly distributed.

[2] Dealer groups, though, will not find themselves in this kind of multiplier position unless all the members of one group also comprise the complete area dealer roster for another manufacturer, which normally would be quite unlikely. Their leverage comes from their strength in numbers. An individual dealer, though, can be a member of many different groups.

TWELVE

DATA CHANNEL ADVERTISING

Probably no other terms in cable create more confusion than *videotex* and *teletext*. Although there are those who tend to use the terms interchangeably, videotex involves a two-way system the viewer can directly interact with on a real-time basis using some form of computer terminal. With teletext, a series of pages is sent in constant rotation to the television set from which the viewer can select and freeze individual pages using a special converter; this control, though, is only at the individual set level and does not communicate directly with the origination point.

There have been many experiments in these two areas using broadcast and telephone distribution as well as cable, but the tremendous equipment costs in getting the terminal hardware into anything approaching a large number of homes makes it unlikely that either will develop into a major factor in advertising in the near future. Already, several on-line text services have been discontinued, and proposed services shelved. However, there is even now a significant potential in local data channel advertising.

Early on at CAB we settled on the term "data channels" to include all forms of video transmission that involve electronically generated text and/or graphics rather than recorded or live action images. While in fact videotex and teletext fall within this category, on a regular, practical basis this term is used to define those channels that use character generators (and sometimes more sophisticated graphics equipment) to present alphanumeric material on local cable channels.

Common uses of these types of channels are for program guides, time-weather and stock ticker displays, and community bulletin boards. Many systems have expanded the bulletin board concept into classified advertising channels similar to the classified advertising pages of newspapers. Frequently data channels will combine information with advertising, either through incorporating simultaneous displays (such as an advertising crawl at the bottom of a time-weather display), or alternating advertising pages with news, sports, or other text material.

USING DATA CHANNELS FOR ADVERTISING

What are some of the reasons you might want to use data channels for advertising?

• *You have a very low advertising budget.* Regular cable advertising is itself inexpensive, but data channels are even more so, especially when you calculate the cost per message exposure. Not only are the ad rates generally low, but there are virtually no production costs. In Muskegon, Michigan, the people handling the data channel sales for the local cable system in 1982 figured that at their rates, the average cost for each message exposure was 2 cents. They subsequently built a whole promotion campaign around the theme, "Get Your 2¢ Worth."

• *You don't need or want video advertising.* Sometimes a full-scale video or slide presentation isn't required, and a message can be adequately conveyed in text form.

• *Frequency of exposure is important.* One significant advantage of a data channel message is that it is cycled and repeated throughout the day. You may find that you prefer spending $25 not for a single 30-second video spot, but for a four-line data channel message that is shown for 15 seconds every five to twenty minutes (depending on the channel traffic) throughout a 48-hour period.

• *You need to make regular changes in ad copy.* It is much easier to rewrite a data channel message than to create a new video spot, and a lot less expensive. Unless there are complex graphics that have to be created in the computer, it takes only a few minutes to type a data channel ad into the appropriate character generator. This means that the text of an ad can be quickly and easily changed at a moment's notice.

• *To supplement regular cable buys.*   Even in cable, situations may arise where you find yourself restricted by commercial length, frequency, or (most likely) production budget limitations in the amount of information that can be included in a video commercial. Data channels can be used to extend the campaign. For example, a retailer might run a regular video spot advertising the store and use a data channel ad to present details about sale items or promotions.

One of the best examples of a business that can benefit from this is a grocery store. While branches of some large supermarket chains can depend on having the parent company produce weekly television commercials showing maybe a half-dozen chainwide specials, most stores have to depend on expensive newspaper ads and circulars once or (more commonly) twice a week to list their specials. This rarely leaves much money to use other advertising. With cable, though, a store can produce a single video commercial that promotes the store in general and is tagged with a message telling viewers to turn to the data channel to see specials; the data channel then has a store ad listing those specials.

Putting together data channel ads is not that much different from designing newspaper ads; in fact, the two can frequently overlap. In many cases, using some graphic elements as well as text can be advantageous in attracting a viewer's attention. When designing your ad, though, be sure you know your parameters first. Videotex and teletext operations tend to use more sophisticated graphics equipment than do local cable data channels. With some systems, such as Telidon, reasonably elaborate artwork can be created and even animated to a certain extent. Other systems, such as Antiope and Prestel, are what is known as alphamosaic, which means they can create pictures by assembling little squares of different colors; since they cannot handle curved or angled lines, though, it is difficult (but not impossible) to create convincing graphics with them.

Most of the character generators used by local systems for their data channels have no graphics capabilities, other than by assembling rough pictures using letters and punctuation marks (sort of like the popular office practice of creating Christmas trees on typewriters or word processors each December). Some character generators, like those made by Texscan/MSI, have a series of "graphics" keys that create different geometric shapes instead of letters; with deft planning, these can be used to create acceptable designs. Advanced character generators, such as the Chyron systems, can make high-quality graphics, but few systems have them available for data channel use. I strongly recommend that if you have any plans to use images other than alphanumeric characters in a data channel ad, you check with the cable system(s) or text service(s) you plan to use as to their capabilities before you take the time to design ads you may not be able to implement.

Beyond the question of graphics, designing a data channel ad can be as easy as writing a newspaper classified ad. Most systems include character/line/page counts in their rate cards; some will even supply you with forms featuring a screen grid with which you can indicate the exact spacing of your text. If you are not given this information initially, ask for it. The number of lines and spaces available per page can vary tremendously depending on the hardware capabilities and the data channel formats laid out by the system. As an example, these are the data channels that one system I profiled had in operation:

> Program guide channel, designed to show a three-hour program schedule in half-hour blocks; includes three pages of advertising, each page consisting of 14 lines of 32 characters.
>
> Sports information channel; includes one page of advertising consisting of 14 lines of 32 characters.
>
> Classified ads channel; includes 32 pages of advertising, sold in full pages (14 lines of 32 characters) or quarter-pages (3 lines of 32 characters).
>
> Stock market quotation channel, featuring horizontal crawls of NYSE and AMEX stock tickers bordering vertical scroll of Dow Jones averages; Dow Jones section alternates with single advertising page of 5 lines of 32 characters.

The system also inserts a single-line, 256-character advertising crawl into the local alphanumeric weather reports it receives in The Weather Channel's network programming.

GENERAL GUIDELINES FOR WRITING ADS

A few general guidelines should be followed in writing data channel ads. First, don't try to pack the screen with as much verbiage as you can fit. With many television sets, text is not always perfectly legible on screen, and depending on how long each page is displayed and how fast the person reads, a viewer may not have sufficient opportunity (or motivation) to decipher a dense block of text.

At the same time, try to avoid extensive use of abbreviations, and use only those in common usage (St., Ave., Lb., Eves., Etc.). Unfamiliar abbreviations can cause confusion or frustration and detract from your message. Admittedly there are many shorthand terms common to print classifieds (6 Rms Riv Vu, SWM, A/C, P/T), but if the reader does not immediately recognize an abbreviation, at least when it is on paper he or she has a chance to mull it over and figure it out. If you find that you need to use a lot of copy in your message, try not to resort to using many abbreviations to force it to fit on one page; a better approach would be to take a second page to complete your message. If you do use more than one page, be sure to indicate that there are additional pages, and try to write your copy so that the viewer will be sufficiently interested to read all of it. Actually, by careful writing and editing, most messages can be effectively expressed on a single page, often with room to spare.

While the choice of character size, font, and color is generally determined by the cable system, in many instances you can select these parameters yourself within the limitations of the hardware and channel format. Using different type sizes, type colors, and background colors can make a fairly ordinary ad seem quite lively. If you are running an ad over a long period of time without any major changes, changing one or more of these features regularly can keep your ad looking fresh. Just a few words of advice here. First, be sure to use contrasting type and background colors for best readability. Light-colored letters on a darker background are easier to read than vice versa, though the latter case can be used to highlight limited areas of text. Avoid using white as a background color, since it does not display well on many television sets and tends to overshadow any text written on it.

CREATIVE USES FOR DATA CHANNELS

While the tendency among people inexperienced in using data channels is to think of them only in terms of routine classified ads, there are many more ways they can be used creatively. One of the advantages mentioned above is that you can change copy easily and frequently, which can be valuable for promotions that depend on constantly changing information. Here are two examples:

• *"Countdown" campaigns.* Organizations such as health club chains often run limited-time membership campaigns several times a year. Retail sales also occur within specified time periods and require constant reminder advertising to build traffic. Data channels are probably the most efficient and least expensive means to run any type of countdown campaign, since it takes only a few seconds to change "Only 5 days left!!" to "Only 4 days left!!", or whatever. These types of promotions can be used for specific sales or for generic purposes, such as the perennial "Only *xx* shopping days until Christmas."

• *Contests.* Data channels can liven up contests or other promotions that otherwise might not even be practical to run in other media. Some possibilities are treasure hunts, puzzles, and trivia contests, in which new clues or questions could be presented on a data channel page every few days. Herald-Leader Telepress, a data channel on the TeleCable system in Lexington, Kentucky, run jointly with the local Knight-Ridder newspaper there, ran a contest in which inserts in the newspaper promoting the cable system and its channels included coupons, the values and places for redemption of which readers had to find out by watching the Telepress channel at given times. Viewer response was reported as "excellent."

A comment frequently heard when discussing data channels is "Come on, no one watches those things."[1] Actually, surveys indicate that consumers will tend to turn to data channels to get information in a hurry; they can turn to a time-weather channel to get a quick update on the weather as they are grabbing their morning coffee, even if they've missed the report on their local radio or television station. Similarly, a viewer can flip on a stock

[1]One videotape rental store ran a data channel ad that began: "So bored with TV you're watching classified ads?"

ticker channel any time of the day to check on prices, while a sports information channel can give a quick rundown of the day's scores before he or she goes to bed without making him or her wait for the 11:22 P.M. report on the local television news. Many viewers also appreciate the overall conciseness of information presented on data channels.

Besides, someone must be watching, since a number of systems, each operating several channels, report that they are not only sold out on most channels, but often have a waiting list of advertisers. They also report success stories such as that of a little-known author promoting a high-priced paperback book with a classified ad on ATC's Manhattan Cable system and having a major New York City bookstore sell out its stock of the title more than five times.

THIRTEEN

POLITICAL ADVERTISING ON CABLE

Political advertising is an area that is becoming increasingly important in cable, as politicians and their campaign strategists recognize the many advantages cable offers them. People tend to think of political advertising in terms of presidential, senatorial, or gubernatorial campaigns, campaigns that cover wide geographic areas. In fact, there are thousands of other political races each year, in which would-be members of Congress, mayors, sheriffs, judges, selectmen, trustees, county clerks, tax assessors, and so on have to appeal to electorates in relatively small areas.

In most cases, local candidates who want to use television advertising are forced to buy time on stations that cover not only their election district or area, but hundreds of square miles outside that area. Since in many instances the area in which a candidate requires coverage coincides with the franchise area of one or more cable systems, the targeting and cost-saving advantages of cable become self-evident.

Some other advantages of cable for political candidates may be a bit less obvious. One is that since more time can be purchased at lower rates than with broadcast television, a political message can be more thorough. Greater emphasis can be placed on addressing issues and stating positions, rather than on trying to create an impressive visual image of the candidate within 30 seconds. Another is that you can usually afford not only to buy more time, but to create a variety of advertisements, enabling you to target different audiences with customized messages. On interactive cable systems, candidates can conduct straw polls of viewer opinions on issues or questions.

A third advantage is that cable audiences are more politically aware and active than the general population. A 1982 study by Simmons Market Research Bureau found that cable households were:

> 19% more likely to have voted in federal, state, or local elections
>
> 32% more likely to have worked actively for a political party and/or candidate
>
> 42% more likely to have engaged in political fundraising
>
> 42% more likely to have written to an elected official about some matter of public business
>
> 54% more likely to have personally visited an elected official to express a point of view

At the first CAB/NCTA Political Advertising Seminar in March 1984, Representative Barney Frank (D-Massachusetts) and political media consultant John Florescu described how Mr. Frank's 1982 election victory against a popular incumbent in a mostly Republican district was won in large part through a cable campaign conducted in Fall River, Massachusetts. The campaign consisted of three half-hour programs produced at the local system in which representatives from each of what had been determined were the key constituencies asked Mr. Frank questions on local issues. Excerpts from the show were later edited into commercials that were aired separately. Also, a series of commercials was made featuring local residents endorsing Mr. Frank (which, as Mr. Florescu pointed out, provided a ready-made phalanx of promotion people for the shows and spots, as the participants were sure to tell everyone they knew to watch them on cable). The entire effort, including production, time costs, and consulting fee, cost less than $10,000.

Another political cable effort Mr. Florescu made in 1982 was for former Massachusetts governor Michael Dukakis, who was then trying to regain his seat and needed to supplement his campaign field organization. Mr. Florescu explained to the campaign organizers that in a caucus contest that depended on party activists, it was more important to reach 4,000 people watching local public affairs programs than 10,000 people watching a Boston College football game. Out of 33 key cities, he identified the 17 that had cable and ran a series of spots on each system's community programming channel. The spots were directed toward political activists and Dukakis supporters and were tagged with a phone number with which viewers could contact the campaign head-quarters to volunteer and to get rides to polling stations. A different phone number was used on each system so that response could be tracked. Spots were also run in cable network local avails to test the response efficiency of each network for political advertising. Mr. Dukakis subsequently swept both the caucus and the election.

There are many considerations of federal law and FCC regulations to be dealt with in using political advertising; in 1982 CAB published a Cable Management Report on the subject that outlined some of these issues, from which the rest of this chapter has been adapted. While staff members of CAB, NCTA, and the FCC cooperated in the preparation of the original report, *neither it nor the following material constitute official pronouncements on the subject by any of these organizations.* The topic is quite complicated, and I cannot hope to cover all the exceptions, qualifications, and interpretations to which the laws and regula-tions are subject. You should be prepared to consult your attorney and the local cable network(s) and system(s) involved if you have any questions about particular uses of cable in a political campaign.

The basic purposes of the federal laws and FCC regulations governing the cablecasting of political announcements on local cable channels[1] are to ensure that:

Candidates for elective office are given or sold reasonable amounts of time for their campaigns

Such candidates are allowed to speak freely without censorship by cable system operators

---

[1] Everything included in this section is equally applicable to cable networks providing time to national candidates, though it is to be expected that virtually all other political advertising would be at the system level.

No discrimination is practiced between competing candidates

The rates charged political candidates are at least as favorable as the rates offered by the system in question to its most favored advertiser(s)

The political cablecasting rules apply to *persons,* by which is meant legally qualified candidates for public office and others speaking either on behalf of or in opposition to such candidates. The much-publicized "fairness doctrine" deals with *issues,* where the broad legal requirement is for a cable system to provide a reasonable opportunity for the presentation of conflicting views on important local public issues of a controversial nature.

Federal law compels a broadcaster to allow a legally qualified candidate for federal elective office (president, vice-president, U.S. senator or U.S. representative) to purchase or be donated reasonable amounts of time on behalf of his or her candidacy. The FCC extends this public service obligation to nonfederal offices, but while a candidate for federal office who seeks access *must* be accommodated, state and local candidates do not have any vested rights, and the broadcaster may exercise its discretion as to whether the particular election is of sufficient local public interest to warrant the sale or donation of political time.

The requirements set out in the preceding paragraph have been previously held by the FCC to apply to cable under section 315(c)(1) of the Communications Act of 1934, as amended, which states that "the term 'broadcasting station' includes a community antenna television system." Despite this, there appears to be some doubt as to whether cable is subject to these requirements, although in the absence of a definitive statement to the contrary by the FCC, the cable industry considers itself covered by the law.

In order to purchase time on a cable system, a legally qualified candidate or his or her supporters must submit a written request for such time. This request must be accepted or rejected by the cable system and then promptly placed in a political file that is to be kept available for public inspection for a period of two years. Requests should include the name and party affiliation of the candidate on whose behalf the request is being made; the election and office involved; the length, cablecast time(s), and rate(s) of the announcement(s) to be run; and the identity of the person(s) and/or organization(s) paying for the spots. Where a committee or other group is purchasing time on behalf of a candidate, the names of the group's officers should also be included. CAB has published a suggested form for such requests that is available on request from cable systems or from CAB.

The sale or donation of time to a candidate by a cable system does not create any obligation to notify opposing candidates of that fact unless it has given the candidate free time within 72 hours of an election. The political file serves as public notice, and the burden is on the opposing candidate to seek the "equal opportunity." Moreover, under the FCC's seven-day rule, any such request must, in order to be honored in full, be made within seven days of the first prior use by the first candidate. Requests made after the required seven days need be honored by the system only with respect to time sold during the immediately preceding seven days; spots cablecast earlier need not be considered in determining to what extent the second request must be accommodated.

It goes without saying that no cable system may discriminate in favor of one qualified candidate over another. This applies both to rates and to equal opportunities with respect to the time being made available. *Equal opportunity* means that opposing candidates requesting it must be given the option to purchase the same amount of time in equally favorable positions as the original user. It is not considered discriminatory, though, if one candidate purchases 10 high-priced prime-time spots and another candidate seeking equal opportunity chooses to purchase 10 lower-priced spots in less favorable time periods; it is discriminatory if the second candidate wants to buy the same prime time spots and the system refuses to sell them to him or her.

In any event, equal opportunity is available only to the actual candidates *for the same office*,[2] not to their supporters, and may be requested only in response to uses by opponents. In order for a program or announcement to constitute a *use* or *appearance* by a legally qualified candidate, the candidate must be the subject of and/or substantially take part in the program or announcement

---

[2]In the case of primaries, this means candidates for the same nomination. A candidate for the Democratic party nomination for an office may request equal opportunity in response to uses by other candidates for that nomination, but not in response to uses by persons who have either won or are seeking the corresponding Republican (or other party) nomination.

in such a way that the audience will recognize his or her picture and/or voice.

The content of the program does not have to be political in nature; for example, broadcasts of Ronald Reagan's old movies would have been considered uses during any of the gubernatorial or presidential elections in which he was a candidate. Similarly, when George Takei ran for a position on the Los Angeles city council, local television stations there rescheduled the airing of certain *Star Trek* episodes in which he played Lt. Sulu, in response to opponents' claims that those telecasts would be considered uses against which they could request time.

However, appearances in bona fide news programming (including on-the-spot coverage of legitimate news events, newscasts, interview shows, and documentaries where the candidate's appearance is incidental to the actual subject thereof) are not considered uses for this purpose. Appearances by a candidate's supporters do not qualify as uses and do not create equal opportunity obligations, although a case might be made that an opposing candidate's supporters have some sort of implied equivalent rights under those circumstances. The use status of cablecast debates can vary depending upon a number of factors, including the identity of the debate sponsor and the timing of the cablecast. It is best for all concerned that a formal determination of this status be obtained in advance of the debate.

By law, a system may not censor the activities of a qualified candidate making an appearance, and is immunized against civil slander or defamation suits arising from such appearance. Where the candidate does not appear, such as where a committee promoting a particular candidate uses the time to ridicule an opponent, that immunity is lost, and the system is therefore afforded the self-protecting right of prescreening tapes or requesting scripts in advance.

If the purchased cablecasts are a use and will run during the 45-day period before a primary election or primary election runoff, or during the 60-day period preceding a general or special election, the charges must not exceed the *lowest* unit charge for the same class and amount of time for the same period. "Lowest" means giving the candidate the benefit of volume discounts (even if the order does not qualify), rates net of agency commissions if no agency is involved, and package plan rates (even if the full volume of spots is not ordered).

Spots running outside the 45- or 60-day rules, or spots not involving a use or appearance by the candidate, may be charged for on the more liberal "comparable use" basis. The system may take into account, for example, the volume of spots ordered, local versus national rates, and other related factors. In any event, candidates must be given the same discounts or privileges given to the system's most favored commercial advertisers under the same circumstances. Note that a cable system may charge less than what is required by law, or even make time available at no charge. Any such benefits extended to one candidate, though, must be extended to all qualified opposing candidates as well. However, if a system is asked to produce political announcements, reasonable production rates may be charged, exclusive of time-based rate restrictions.

All paid political advertisements or programs must include announcements identifying the actual sponsor thereof; a person buying political time as an agent must identify his or her principal(s) in the sponsorship announcement. Such announcements must include the words "paid for," "sponsored by," or "furnished by," and in the case of cablecasts over five minutes in length, the announcement must be given both at the beginning and the end of the program. Federal candidates are also responsible for indicating within any cablecast on their behalf whether or not they have authorized it, as required by the Federal Election Campaign Act.

FOURTEEN

CABLE ADVERTISING STANDARDS AND PRACTICES

As an essentially closed-circuit medium, cable is not bound by most of the restrictions broadcasters have had to deal with, including restrictions on advertising. There has been considerable interest, therefore, in the question of how cable will handle controversial areas such as liquor and cigarette advertising, neither of which are permitted in broadcasting, as well as certain other products not allowed on the air.

LIQUOR AND CIGARETTES

To begin with, it is a common misconception that liquor advertising is prohibited from the airwaves by the FCC. In fact, the absence of liquor advertising on television and radio is the result of a self-policing decision by the liquor industry itself. Presumably industry members felt that, while wine and beer are mild enough, they did not want to run the risk of encouraging impressionable youngsters who might see their commercials to try "the hard stuff" at too early an age. Cigarette advertising, on the other hand, was specifically banned from the airwaves by Congress in 1971. The question often posed is this: Since cable is not a broadcast medium, isn't it exempt from these regulations, and why shouldn't it be used to advertise liquor and cigarettes?

Liquor advertising has indeed appeared on cable. The most noted occurrence (and the only one on network that I know of) was in 1981, when Remy Martin sponsored a series of programs on Telefrance-USA. Preceding each of these programs was a 2½-minute infomercial with the president of Remy Martin describing the Cognac region of France and the manufacture and tradition of cognac, ending by saying how pleased the company is to sponsor the series. This infomercial, which did not really advertise the cognac itself and which ran only a few times, acquired a life of its own due to its fame as "cable's big liquor ad." I have also seen a few local cable ads for individual liquor stores, rather than for actual beverages, which in and of itself is a grey area.

As a practical matter, though, while the cable industry takes the position that it is not technically bound by the broadcasters' restrictions, it feels morally bound to respect the decisions that led to these particular restraints. Also, no system or network really wants to be the guinea pig that runs a commercial and ends up fighting a lengthy court battle when either the government or outraged citizens makes it prove it is allowed to run the spot.

In Oklahoma, for example, a bill was passed several years ago that not only prohibited systems from running liquor ads, but also required them to monitor all cable network and broadcast signals they received from outside the state and block out any liquor commercials. Aside from the sheer impracticality of complying with the demands of this bill, there were also major First Amendment, FCC regulation, and copyright infringement issues involved. When challenged in court, the legality of the bill was alternately upheld and overturned in a series of appeals, until the U.S. Supreme Court delivered its landmark decision in the case in June 1984. The court not only overturned the Oklahoma bill, but went on to reaffirm that the FCC has both independent jurisdiction to regulate cable and broad authority to preempt nonfederal regulations pertaining to most operational aspects of cable. In other words, the FCC can, if it chooses, overturn any state or municipal restrictions on cable systems' activities, including any restrictions on advertising.

The National Association of Broadcasters (NAB) established the Television Code in 1952, which stood as a self-regulatory benchmark until 1982, when the NAB suspended it in response to suits brought by the U.S. Justice Department. The cable industry has on various occasions attempted to come up with its own code of standards but has yet to do so; given the ruling on the NAB code, it may never be able to.

Most cable networks, however, like their broadcast counterparts, have their own internal standards and practices guidelines. Some are clearly stated, others are unspoken but understood; in either case, they are designed not as censoring tools, but as protective devices to exclude clearly unacceptable materials. For example, MTV: Music Television, which has a large teen and preteen audience in addition to the 18-to-35 market, excludes not only cigarettes and liquor (though permitting beer), but also gambling, dating services, drug-related paraphernalia, birth control devices, and X-rated film and video products.

LINGERIE AND LESS

The last item leads to the inevitable discussion of X-rated advertising in general. Despite the fact that a few notorious New York City local public access shows have somehow become for many people the sum total of what cable television is all about, the cable industry as a whole is very much against the use of X-rated material in its programming and advertising. Even most of the "adult entertainment" services, such as The Playboy Channel, restrict themselves to "hard R" rather than true "X" programming, although ads of the latter nature have been seen on some public access shows.[1] So if you plan to use any daring material in your cable commercials, I suggest you check with the network(s) and/or system(s) you plan to run them on to make sure they will be accepted.

This is not to say that cable is entirely unwilling to take chances or break new ground in controversial areas. Earlier I

[1]Even so, when a producer from one New York City TV station's news department called CAB in 1982 for assistance in doing a story on "new advertising opportunities in cable," it quickly became clear that she was actually determined to do a story on X-rated commercials (although to her credit, she finally toned down that aspect and spent most of the story describing other types of cable advertising after I redirected her research).

mentioned the Budweiser commercial where people were shown actually drinking the beer; this led to a number of articles in some advertising trade publications speculating on the effect this would have on advertising standards. Front-page news was made when Ce Soir introduced a 10-second lingerie spot on cable showing a woman clad only in a bra and bikini brief. While in fact there was more cloth in the underwear than there appears to be in some of the swimsuits worn in some soft drink commercials (not to mention in many daytime and primetime shows), the fact that for the first time a woman was shown wearing lingerie without other clothing under it was enough to send shock waves through the advertising industry. This is an example of how advertisers have been able to use cable to escape the artificial restrictions of broadcast television to demonstrate their product in a more realistic and practical way, while being no more offensive than the Sunday *New York Times Magazine*.

That effort, however, did pave the way for a much more risque commercial that appeared on the scene two years later. Berlei USA introduced a spot that featured an unclad young woman (shown from a back view) putting on a set of underwear while moaning sensuously about how much she liked the feel of silk against her skin. Although there was no side or frontal nudity, the intended eroticism came through loud and clear. To put it in perspective, though, when this spot was shown at a panel discussion at the 1984 CAB Cable Advertising Conference, it was greeted with chuckles rather than horrified gasps from the audience.

The lesson in all this is that for the most part cable offers freedom, but not license. Feel free to be adventuresome, but keep in mind that while cable people do not mind breaking down some of the artificial barriers set up by the television industry, they still try to operate within the boundaries of good taste and responsibility toward viewers.

FIFTEEN

A LOOK AT THE FUTURE OF CABLE

In talking about the future of cable, there are many who will say that it will be wiped out, or at least stopped in its tracks, by competing technologies. To give you a little perspective on this issue, let me explain these technologies and discuss the implications of each.

SATELLITE MASTER ANTENNA TELEVISION (SMATV)

Most apartment buildings, particularly those built in the last 30 years, have some form of master television antenna that provides reception for all the apartments. This type of system is known as master antenna television (MATV). SMATV is identical to this except that the antenna is a satellite earth station rather than a standard FM antenna; it essentially converts the apartment house into a miniature cable system. Until recently, it could deliver only a few channels, but new systems are being developed with much greater channel capacity. More important, since the FCC preempted state and local regulatory authority over SMATV, it can be installed much more quickly and does not have to pay franchise fees or otherwise deal with any municipal agency. (It does, however, have to get authorization to pick up each satellite signal from the respective networks.) Also, landlords can make deals for portions of SMATV revenues, deals they are not allowed to make with cable systems, and so are likely to be even less inclined to allow cable in their buildings.

Because of this, there is some concern that SMATV could be used to pick up the most desirable locations in major markets before cable would get through the franchising process, and leave the lesser pickings for cable. Actually, multiresidence units represent a relatively small part of the cable business, and only about 3 percent of total U.S. households are in SMATV-serviceable dwellings, so the overall effect should not be major. Even so, a few cable companies are talking about installing interim SMATV facilities in buildings within their franchise areas where they have not yet built their systems. When they do reach the building with cable, they would remove the SMATV antenna and plug in the cable.

MULTIPOINT DISTRIBUTION SYSTEMS (MDS)

MDS has been around for a while in noncable cities, usually providing pay cable services before cable shows up. Most have delivered only one channel, though technological advances are promising up to a dozen channels. Again, the issue of price versus value comes up, since cable can provide more channels for the same or less cost. Although leading MDS operators say that they would like to coexist with cable, the likelihood is that it will be a head-to-head battle.

SUBSCRIPTION TELEVISION (STV)

STV, basically, is over-the-air pay television. A UHF television station transmits a scrambled broadcast signal, and subscribers who pay a monthly fee receive a decoding device that enables them to view the service. While STV companies use as a key selling point the fact that you do not need cable for their service, there are several disadvantages to STV. One is that as a broadcast signal it is subject to the same reception vagaries that may affect other signals in the market; in other words, if you cannot get good reception with your TV antenna, you're out of luck.

Also, you usually pay for a single channel at least as much, if not more, than you would pay on most cable systems for full basic service plus one pay service. Although some studies have shown that cable has a hard time in areas where STV has gotten a foothold, once STV subscribers see the economic and service benefits of cable, it is likely that they will in fact switch over.

DIRECT BROADCAST SATELLITE (DBS)

Another system often touted as a major competitor to cable is direct broadcast satellite (DBS), which would bypass cable systems and deliver signals from a satellite directly to a satellite antenna in the home.

While DBS will definitely be a participant in the new electronic media, it is not likely to have any noticeable effect on cable or cable advertising. To begin with, it is not yet as simple as sticking a pie-plate-size antenna out your bedroom window. Currently, in order to pick up satellite transmissions clearly, you need an antenna considerably larger than that, though as newer satellites that are more powerful in their retransmission capabilities are launched, the size of the antenna needed may be reduced. Also, with any antenna, you have to be able to point it directly at the satellite with no obstructions (buildings, mountains) in the way.

DBS service is expected to provide only four or five channels. In 1983, over 80 percent of cable subscribers received a minimum of 20 channels, with three-fourths of those receiving 30 or more channels. Even with the eventual economies of scale that may be reached in DBS equipment, a basic rig could cost the same as several years of subscribing to cable, while giving far less service.

DBS's future really will be in those areas where cable will not go, such as isolated small towns with few homes or where individual homes may be separated by miles, where it is not practical or cost-efficient for a cable company to string the wires necessary to serve those homes.

LOW-POWER TELEVISION (LPTV)

The mere presence of LPTV in a market is not likely-to affect the introduction or expansion of cable in a market, since it is simply one more broadcast channel. The LPTV stations already in operation have relatively little influence in their markets. Where LPTV might become an issue is in its competition with a cable system's local programming, since by definition it is a highly localized medium. Unless it can offer programming competitive with other broadcast and cable networks, it must concentrate on a local basis.

One thing to keep in mind is that LPTV stations do not have to be carried on cable systems under the FCC's must-carry rules, which means that unless the rules are changed or the cable system chooses (or is pressured) to add a station to the system, LPTV will be received only in noncable households or in cable households that are willing to change cable and antenna leads on their sets whenever they want to watch it. To that extent, it should not have any effect on the cable audience. In fact, the most likely conflict will be if a situation arises where the cable system and the LPTV station have a disagreement over the rights to cover a particular event, such as a local sports tournament.

The most important point to keep in mind is that all these technologies will be playing catch-up to cable. The growth of cable that is taking place now will effectively inhibit the introduction of most other services. Even if cable reaches only the projections indicated on page 2, that will still represent a major force in the U.S. Another thing to note is that SMATV, MDS, and DBS companies are all talking about offering cable networks, including the advertiser-supported ones as at least part of their programming, so network cable advertisers could find themselves with a bonus audience beyond the cable universe.

CHICKEN LITTLE VISITS CABLE

Meanwhile, people point to the various closings and mergers of cable networks that have occurred, as well as the franchising problems faced by Warner Amex and other cable operators, as evidence of a bleak future for cable. It's about time some misunderstandings were corrected. To begin with, the failures of CBS Cable and Satellite News Channel were due not to any inherent fault in cable, but in large part to errors in judgment and unrealistic expectations. The same type of expectations are what have caused so many of the existing franchise problems; cable operators have promised and/or municipalities have demanded services and amenities not economically feasible to provide. Now that most of the "blue sky" period of cable has passed and it is starting to be looked at, both inside and outside the industry, as an established business, we should begin to see more reasonable franchises being negotiated (and more advertising contracts), and a more rapid expansion of cable as a result.

The mergers of various networks, such as Cable Health Network and Daytime, and Showtime and The Movie Channel, have strengthened the companies involved by streamlining operations, cutting losses, and providing more resources for obtaining programming and building subscribership. Similarly, the merger of ARTS with The Entertainment Channel (the closing of the latter was due in part to its inability to shake off the cultural cable label it had been tagged with in the press) has resulted in a broader range and schedule of offerings with less repetition.

Churn, or subscriber turnover, is also wrongly cited as another sign of a dim future for cable. To begin with, it is primarily an issue regarding pay cable. Churn does not so much involve complete disconnects as it does switching or downgrading of pay service. This often results from systems selling new subscribers their complete package of pay services and the subscribers subsequently dropping those which either do not interest them or substantially duplicate other services.

Churn also comes from transients, which is an uncontrollable factor faced by any household service, and disconnects initiated by the system for lack of subscriber payment. There is very little voluntary basic cable disconnect. It is probably less of a problem in cable than in, say, print media, which also have to deal with subscribers who cancel, let lapse, or do not pay for their subscriptions. Another thing to consider is that given the problem of piracy, which is a problem not only for cable but for other electronic media as well, the actual number of cable viewers is probably higher than reported subscribership would indicate.

THE FUTURE OF CABLE

Now that we have looked at the various reasons why cable won't make it, let's take a look at what is more likely to occur.

• *Cable systems.*   Cable systems will continue to be built, although not with the hundreds of channels that were once expected to become standard. More likely both municipalities and cable companies will go into the franchise process with more realistic expectations on both sides. We can also expect to see continued rebuilding and upgrading of older systems to expand their channel capacities and hence their ability to offer more cable-originated programming.

• *Cable networks.*   Most of the services currently operative will probably remain so over the near term, although some of the marginal ones may not be able to capitalize themselves adequately over a long period of time and may be forced to fold. There will probably be several other networks launched, and only time will tell which networks will still be around ten years from now.

While many of the networks are still operating in the red, it is important to keep in mind that cable is an industry that requires a great deal of money both up front and on an ongoing basis, and that it takes many years to even begin to break even. Those companies that can afford to ride out the initial loss period will probably survive and do quite well. Those who either can't or won't support their early efforts won't make it.[1]

• *Advertising on pay cable services.*   It is almost de rigeur to hear uninitiated people, viewers and advertisers alike, say "Cable television advertising? Hey, wait a minute, I thought cable TV meant 'no commercials'!" Once I've gotten over the hurdle of

---

[1] I might point out that it took the ABC television network twenty years to become profitable, and that the same company that shut down *TV-Cable Week* after a few months also kept a major money-loser called *Sports Illustrated* going for eight years before it began to show a profit.

explaining the difference between pay cable service and advertiser-supported cable services, the next question, either in anticipation or concern is: "Okay, when is HBO [or whomever] going to start taking ads?" In response to that question, most of the pay networks offering movies and entertainment continue to hold their ground, insisting they will never accept advertising.

A major factor in that argument is the feeling that subscribers have bought cable to avoid commercials and will not stand for them. Actually, studies have shown that not only isn't the avoidance of commercials a high priority element in people's decisions to purchase cable, but that many subscribers would not object to the inclusion of a limited number of commercials *between* programs if it kept their subscription costs down.

So far, the pay cable services have been able to pass their own cost increases along to subscribers. Eventually, though, they will reach a price level at which they encounter consumer resistance. Then the only means of maintaining both service quality and subscriber levels may be by replacing some of their on-air promotion (which is really advertising for themselves) with outside advertising. Given the length of the breaks between many movies shown on the pay services, it is possible that such a development may provide advertisers another opportunity to effectively use infomercials, rather than one more place to run their 30-second broadcast television spots.

Several regional pay sports networks such as Sportschannel and Sports Time Cable Network already accept advertising, and they may be worth looking into if for some reason the advertiser-supported services cannot meet your needs. However, I would not recommend writing up your media plans with allocations for the major nonsports pay cable services yet.

WHAT DOES IT ALL MEAN FOR THE ADVERTISER?

While we are busy worrying about the future of cable, the most important point to keep in mind is that cable is here *today*. It is something that you can use now and that you can get results with now. When you are looking to advertise this year's line of new cars, the opening of your new restaurant next month, your next

Columbus Day sale, or next weekend's garage sale, it doesn't matter whether or not a particular network or show will still be around five years from now. The investment you make in cable advertising is one that can pay off for you today.

When you come right down to it, hardware advances and competitive media are not the issue. After all, you are not making a capital investment or purchasing equipment that you hope to use for the next ten years. The real key to cable's growth or lack thereof is going to be better programming, and here we're dealing with something of a vicious circle. Cable needs good programming. Good programming costs money. To get money, cable has to sell advertising. Advertisers only want to buy into good programming. Good programming costs money. To get money, cable has to. . . .

In Chapter 8 I talked about advertisers producing and sponsoring custom-made programming. This is an area advertisers should continue to explore. Advertisers can create not only the commercials they want, but also the environments they want to show those commercials in, all at affordable rates providing a favorable cost-benefit ratio.

There are many readily available sources of programming ideas. Cable is often compared to specialized magazines. A number of magazines have produced or had others produce cable shows based on their content or format (*American Baby, Women's Day, Better Homes and Gardens, Good Housekeeping,* and others). Given the number of magazines on the market, there are many still available for use.

I believe we are seeing with cable in the eighties the same thing that happened to television in the fifties. Then too, many people were predicting failure for the new medium, some of them just wishing it would just go away. Meantime, far-sighted advertisers invested in the new medium and saw their investments pay off as the medium grew to the point where now it is so much a part of American life that most people under the age of 30 cannot imagine there ever was a time when there was no television or television advertising. A few years from now, we will probably look at cable and wonder why everyone made such a fuss about such an ordinary household fixture.

APPENDIX A

HOW CABLE WORKS

Were Marshall McLuhan alive today, he would probably agree that cable has become an area where the medium is more often the message than is the real message. As I mentioned earlier, it is not necessary for you to understand all the electronic workings of cable in order to use cable advertising any more than you have to understand the theory behind offset web printing in order to use magazine advertising. For those of you who may be interested, though, here is a simple primer on how cable works.

Cable systems provide subscribers with four basic types of programming: satellite services, regular broadcast television, distant broadcast television, and local origination programming.

Satellite services are usually cable networks, both advertiser-supported and pay. The network sends its program signal to an uplink facility that transmits it to a satellite orbiting 22,300 miles above the earth. The satellite is said to be in a geosynchronous or geostationary orbit, because at that distance its orbit keeps it above the same spot on earth at all times. On the satellite, an electronic device called a transponder picks up the signal, amplifies it, and retransmits it back to earth in a broad pattern that covers the whole country (not to mention parts of Canada, Mexico, and the Caribbean). The cable system picks up the signal with an earth

139

station, which consists of an antenna (also known as a dish, since most tend to be dish-shaped) and the necessary receiving equipment.

Regular television signals are picked up using antennas similar to those used by homes, although more sensitive. Distant broadcast signals, that is, television signals from outside the television market in which the system is located, are generally distributed and received by microwave relays.

Local origination in this sense refers to anything originating at the system, not picked up from an outside signal. This would include programming produced by the system, access programming, or outside syndicated programming shown by the system, all of which is fed directly from the system's control room.

All these various signals are fed into the headend, where they are processed and sent out along the trunk cable, which is usually strung along telephone or utility poles, but may also be run underground. Amplifiers are installed at regular intervals to ensure that the proper signal strength is maintained throughout the system. From drop boxes attached to the trunk cable, drop cables are run into subscribers' homes. The drop cable is connected to a converter, which translates the cable signal into a standard television signal and acts as a channel selector for the viewer. A short length of drop cable connects the cable converter to the television set (in cases where the subscriber has a cable-ready set compatible with the system hardware, the drop cable is connected directly to the set without a converter being used).

Since pay cable signals are meant to be seen only by those households specifically subscribing to and paying for the service, those signals are scrambled before being fed into subscribers' homes. There are a number of methods for doing this. One is by means of a scrambler in the drop box, which the cable installer has to adjust manually for each subscriber. Another is to scramble the signal at the headend, and provide pay subscribers with decoders which are then installed either inside or adjacent to their converter(s). A third method, which is in use in some systems, involves a concept called addressability, in which special converters are used throughout the system and a computer at the headend can selectively address each converter and tell it which channels to let through and which to scramble.

APPENDIX B

ADVERTISER-SUPPORTED CABLE NETWORKS

The following is a basic list of the national satellite-distributed networks that accept advertising. The information is accurate as of January 1, 1985, though due to the constantly changing nature of the cable industry, complete accuracy cannot be guaranteed after that point. For up-to-date information, contact the individual networks or **CAB**. All times shown are Eastern.

ARTS & ENTERTAINMENT NETWORK (A&E)

555 Fifth Avenue
New York, NY 10017
(212) 661-4500

Arts&Entertainment Network

Ad Sales Offices in: New York

Hours: Monday–Sunday, 8 A.M.–4 A.M. (full-day service)
Monday–Sunday, 8 P.M.–4 A.M. (evening service)

Ad Avails per Hour: Network: 5 minutes
Local: 1 minute

Programming Description: An international array of music, dance, films, Broadway plays, opera, and documentaries on everything artistic, plus exclusive drama, adventure, and comedy programs from the BBC.

BLACK ENTERTAINMENT TELEVISION (BET)

1232 31st Street, NW
Washington, DC 20007
(202) 337-5260

Ad Sales Offices in: Washington, New York

Hours: Monday–Sunday, 8 P.M.–2 A.M.

Ad Avails per Hour: Network: 8 minutes
Local: 2 minutes

Programming Description: Black-oriented sports, entertainment, and family programming.

BUSINESS TIMFS

727 Eleventh Avenue
New York, NY 10019
(212) 247-7030

BUSINESS TIMES

Ad Sales Offices in: New York, San Francisco, Boston, Chicago, Dallas

Hours: Monday–Friday, 6 A.M.–8 A.M.

Ad Avails per Hour: Network: 10 minutes
Local: 2 minutes

Programming Description: An early-morning business news roundup for executives containing reports and analysis of key economic and financial news of the day, profiles of leading business figures, sports and weather.

CABLE NEWS NETWORK (CNN)

1050 Techwood Drive NW
Atlanta, GA 30318
(404) 827-1500

Ad Sales Offices in: Atlanta, New York, Chicago, Detroit, Los
Angeles

Hours: Monday–Sunday, 24 hours

Ad Avails per Hour: Network: 9 minutes
Local: 3 minutes

Programming Description: National and international news,
interviews, business news, sports and
weather.

CBN CABLE NETWORK

1000 Centerville Turnpike
Virginia Beach, VA 23463
(804) 424-7777

Ad Sales Offices in: New York, Chicago, Dallas, Los Angeles

Hours: Monday–Sunday, 24 hours

Ad Avails per Hour: Network: 11 minutes
Local: Averages 1 minute

Programming Description: Family-oriented entertainment programming. Includes daily movies,
westerns, classic comedies, game
shows, Christian inspirational programming, etc.

CNN HEADLINE NEWS

1050 Techwood Drive NW
Atlanta, GA 30318
(404) 827-1500

Ad Sales Offices in: Atlanta, New York, Chicago, Detroit, Los
Angeles

Hours: Monday–Sunday, 24 hours

Ad Avails per Hour: Network: 10 minutes
Local: 3 minutes, 20 seconds

Programming Description: 24-hour news headline service in up-
dated half-hour cycles.

COUNTRY MUSIC TELEVISION (CMTV)

30 East 40th Street, Suite 507
New York, NY 10016
(212) 686-4340

Ad Sales Offices in: New York

Hours: Monday–Sunday, 24 hours

Ad Avails per Hour: Network: 7 minutes
Local: 3 minutes

Programming Description: 24 hours of pure country music: videos,
concerts, and specials, plus news and
interviews with country music artists.

ENTERTAINMENT AND SPORTS PROGRAMMING NETWORK (ESPN)

ESPN Plaza
935 Middle Street
Bristol, CT 06010
(203) 584-8477

Ad Sales Offices in: New York, Chicago, Los Angeles

Hours: Monday–Sunday, 24 hours

Ad Avails per Hour: Network: Averages 8 minutes in prime time;
6 minutes, 10 seconds otherwise
Local: Averages 2 minutes in prime time; 3
minutes, 50 seconds otherwise

Programming Description: Live and taped professional and college sports, sports news and inter-
views, plus Business Times.

FINANCIAL NEWS NETWORK (FNN)

2525 Ocean Park Boulevard
Santa Monica, CA 90405
(213) 450-2412

Ad Sales Offices in: New York, Chicago, Los Angeles, Miami

Hours: Monday–Friday, 6 A.M.–7 P.M.

Ad Avails per Hour: Network: 8 minutes
Local: 4 minutes

Programming Description: Business and financial news, political and economic analysis.

LIFETIME

1211 Avenue of the Americas
New York, NY 10036
(212) 719-7230

Ad Sales Offices in: New York, Chicago, Los Angeles

Hours: Monday–Sunday, 24 hours

Ad Avails per Hour: Network: 9 minutes
Local: 2 minutes

Programming Description: Lifestyle, health, and science programming designed to enrich and enhance viewers' lives.

MSN—THE INFORMATION CHANNEL

Modern Satellite Network
5000 Park Street North
St. Petersburg, FL 33709
(813) 541-7571

Ad Sales Offices in: New York, Chicago, San Francisco, Washington

Hours: Monday–Friday, 10 A.M.–1 P.M.

Ad Avails per Hour: Network: 4 minutes
Local: 2 minutes

Programming Description: A variety of informational programming for consumers, including *The Home Shopping Show* and programs on travel, business, self-improvement, and entertainment.

MTV: MUSIC TELEVISION

1133 Avenue of the Americas
New York, NY 10036
(212) 944-5380

Ad Sales Offices in: New York, Chicago, Detroit, Los Angeles, Atlanta

Hours: Monday–Sunday, 24 hours

Ad Avails per Hour: Network: 6 minutes
Local: 2 minutes

Programming Description: Contemporary music videos in stereo. Weekly concerts, music news, interviews with major recording artists.

THE NASHVILLE NETWORK (TNN)

2806 Opryland Drive
Nashville, TN 37214
(615) 889-6840

Ad Sales Offices in: New York, Chicago, Los Angeles, Atlanta, Dallas

Hours: Monday–Sunday, 9 A.M.–3 A.M.

Ad Avails per Hour: Network: 10 minutes
Local: 2 minutes

Programming Description: 18-hour-a-day entertainment service with a country music emphasis.

NATIONAL CHRISTIAN NETWORK (NCN)

1150 West King Street
Cocoa, FL 32922
(305) 632-1000

No network ad sales offices

Hours: Monday–Sunday, 24 hours

Ad Avails per Hour: Network: None
Local: 1 minute

Programming Description: Multidenominational religious programming.

NATIONAL JEWISH TELEVISION (NJT)

2621 Palisade Avenue
Riverdale, NY 10463
(212) 549-4160

Ad Sales Offices in: Riverdale

Hours: Sunday, 1 P.M.-4 P.M.

Ad Avails per Hour: Network: 8 minutes
Local: 2 minutes

Programming Description: Programming for the Jewish community, including news, public affairs, cultural and religious programs.

NICKELODEON

1133 Avenue of the Americas
New York, NY 10036
(212) 944-5481

Ad Sales Offices in: New York

Hours: Monday–Sunday, 7 A.M.-8 P.M.

Ad Avails per Hour: Network: 7 minutes (8:30 A.M.-3 P.M.: 4 minutes)
Local: 1 minute

Programming Description: Entertainment and educational programming for young people ages 2–15.

SATELLITE PROGRAM NETWORK (SPN)

8252 South Harvard
Tulsa, OK 74137
(918) 481-0881

Mailing Address: PO Box 470684
Tulsa, OK 74147

Ad Sales Offices in: Tulsa, New York, Chicago, Los Angeles

Hours: Monday–Sunday, 24 hours

Ad Avails per Hour: Network: 12 minutes
Local: 2 minutes

Programming Description: Lifestyle programming, consisting of business, health-related, informational, entertainment, music, sports, and international programming, blocked into dayparts by program type.

SIN TELEVISION NETWORK

460 West 42nd Street
New York, NY 10036
(212) 502-1300

Ad Sales Offices in: New York, Chicago, Detroit, Los Angeles, Dallas, Miami

Hours: Monday–Sunday, 24 hours

Ad Avails per Hour: Network: 7 minutes
                    Local: None

Programming Description: Spanish-language programming, including movies, live sports, children's shows, comedies, novelas, miniseries, variety shows, specials, and a national weeknightly newscast from Miami.

USA CABLE NETWORK

208 Harristown Road
Glen Rock, NJ 07452
(201) 445-8550

Ad Sales Offices in: New York, Chicago, Los Angeles

Hours: Monday–Sunday, 24 hours

Ad Avails per Hour: Network: 10 minutes
                    Local: 2 minutes

Programming Description: Live sports events, sports news, and interview shows; children's entertainment/educational programming; women's entertainment/family service programming; documentary/entertainment programming; young adult programming.

VIDEO HITS ONE (VH-1)

1133 Avenue of the Americas
New York, NY 10036
(212) 944-5380

Ad Sales Offices in: New York, Chicago, Detroit, Los Angeles, Atlanta

Hours: Monday–Sunday, 24 hours

Ad Avails per Hour: Network: 4 minutes
Local: 2 minutes

Programming Description: Contemporary music videos in stereo and entertainment news, programmed for the 25–34 market.

THE WEATHER CHANNEL

2480 Mount Wilkinson Parkway, Suite 200
Atlanta, GA 30339
(404) 434-6800

Ad Sales Offices in: New York, Chicago

Hours: Monday–Sunday, 24 hours

Ad Avails per Hour: Network: 10 minutes
Local: 2 minutes; also one-line alphanumeric crawl during local forecasts, 45–50 seconds 12 times each hour

Programming Description: National, regional, and local weather reports/forecasts and weather-related features.

WGN-TV

2501 Bradley Place
Chicago, IL 60618
(312) 528-2311

Ad Sales Offices in: Chicago; also represented by Blair Television

Hours: Monday–Sunday, 24 hours

Ad Avails per Hour: Network: 9 minutes
Local: None

Programming Description: Chicago independent television station.

WOR-TV

1440 Broadway
New York, NY 10018
(212) 764-7000

Ad Sales Offices in: New York, Secaucus (NJ); also represented by
Blair Television

Hours: Monday–Sunday, 24 hours

Ad Avails per Hour: Network: 12 minutes
Local: None

Programming Description: Secaucus, NJ, independent television
station.

WPIX-TV

220 East 42nd Street
New York, NY 10017
(212) 949-1100

Ad Sales Offices in: New York; also represented by TeleRep Inc.

Hours: Monday–Sunday, 24 hours

Ad Avails per Hour: Network: 16 minutes (8 P.M.–11 P.M.: 14
minutes)
Local: None

Programming Description: New York independent television
station.

SUPERSTATION WTBS

1050 Techwood Drive NW
Atlanta, GA 30318
(404) 827-1717

Ad Sales Offices in: Atlanta, New York, Chicago, Detroit, Los
Angeles

Hours: Monday–Sunday, 24 hours

Ad Avails per Hour: Network: 9 minutes, 30 seconds
Local: None

Programming Description: Atlanta independent television station with emphasis on family programming, sports, situation comedies, movies.

APPENDIX C

FURTHER SOURCES
OF INFORMATION

TRADE ASSOCIATIONS

CABLETELEVISION ADVERTISING BUREAU, INC.

767 Third Avenue
New York, NY 10017
(212) 751-7770

CAB is a cable industry trade association whose purpose is to develop cable as an advertising medium by providing information to the advertising community and sales training and assistance to cable systems, networks, and sales representatives.

NATIONAL CABLE TELEVISION ASSOCIATION INC.

1724 Massachusetts Avenue NW
Washington, DC 20036
(202) 775-3550

NCTA is a cable industry trade association dealing with public policy issues, programming, marketing, engineering, and operational aspects of the industry.

CABLE TELEVISION ADMINISTRATION & MARKETING SOCIETY, INC.

219 Perimeter Center Parkway, Suite 480
Atlanta, GA 30346
(404) 399-5574

CTAM is a professional society that deals with key management and marketing issues in the cable industry by providing a forum for idea exchange.

COUNCIL FOR CABLE INFORMATION

126 East 56th Street
New York, NY 10022
(212) 308-7060

The Council for Cable Information is a cable industry trade association established in 1983 to cultivate positive consumer attitudes toward cable as a unique beneficial service to the home and the community.

CABLE- AND ADVERTISING-RELATED PERIODICALS

Cablevision.   Titsch Communications Inc., 2500 Curtis Street, Suite 2500, Denver, CO 80205. Published weekly.

Multichannel News.   Fairchild Publications, a division of Capital Cities Media, Inc., 7 East 12th Street, New York, NY 10003. Published weekly.

The two leading newsweeklies of the cable industry. Indispensible for keeping up with cable industry news and developments.

Cable Age.   Television Editorial Corp. Publication Office, 1270 Avenue of the Americas, New York, NY 10020. Published bi-weekly.

Another major source of information about the cable industry. Tends to focus on feature and analysis pieces more than up-to-the-minute news items.

Cable Marketing.   Associated Cable Enterprises, Inc., a division of Jobson Publishing Corp., 352 Park Avenue South, New York, NY 10010. Published monthly.

Designed primarily for network and system subscriber marketing personnel, but also covers advertising and other cable subjects.

Cable Television Business, formerly **TVC.** Cardiff Publishing Company, a subsidiary of Cardiff Communications, Inc., 6530 South Yosemite Street, Englewood, CO 80111. Published semi-monthly.

Tends to lean toward financial, technical, and franchise interests as a rule, though it has done some major features on cable advertising.

Cable TV Advertising. Paul Kagan Associates, Inc., 26386 Carmel Rancho Lane, Carmel, CA 93923. Published semi-monthly.

One of more than two dozen newsletters and publications covering various aspects of the cable industry published by one of its leading researchers. Expensive but recommended; often uncovers news or other interesting items before the other trade publications do.

View. View Communications Corp., 150 East 58th Street, New York, NY 10155. Published monthly.

Primarily covers matters relating to cable programming, though also covers other aspects of the industry, including cable advertising.

Broadcasting. Broadcasting Publications Inc., 1735 DeSales Street, Washington, DC 20036. Published weekly.

The leading magazine of the broadcasting industry. Includes a small weekly section on cable and also covers major stories (mostly regulation-related).

Television/Broadcast Communications. Globecom Publishing Limited, 4121 West 83rd Street, Suite 265, Prairie Village, KS 66208. Published monthly.

A technically oriented magazine for broadcasters, it also features a quarterly supplement called *Access to Cable Communications* geared toward cable production (including advertising).

Advertising Age. Crain Communications Inc., 740 Rush Street, Chicago, IL 60611. Published weekly.

Electronic Media. Crain Communications Inc., 740 Rush Street, Chicago, IL 60611. Published weekly.

The leading magazine of the advertising industry. Has been a leader in reporting on and advocating cable advertising, evidenced in part by its spinning off and enlarging its coverage of the new electronic media into a separate magazine. Indispensable.

Adweek. A/S/M Communications, Inc., 820 Second Avenue, New York, NY 10017. Five regional editions, published weekly.

Compact and easy-to-read advertising news magazine, but tends to be occasionally off the mark as far as cable goes.

Madison Avenue. Madison Avenue Magazine Publishing Corp., 369 Lexington Avenue, New York, NY 10017. Published monthly.

Marketing Communications.   United Business Publications, Inc., a subsidiary of Media Horizons, Inc., 475 Park Avenue South, New York, NY 10016. Published monthly.

Marketing & Media Decisions.   Decisions Publications, Inc., 1140 Avenue of the Americas, New York, NY 10036. Published monthly, plus two additional issues.

Three fine advertising magazines, all with regular coverage of the cable industry and relevant developments.

GLOSSARY OF CABLE AND RELATED ADVERTISING TERMS

Advertisers have often expressed concern about "not knowing the cable language." A lot of the language in question deals with technical or regulatory matters not related to cable advertising. Nevertheless, in working with cable you may run across some unfamiliar terms, but this glossary should help make things clearer. Note that some of these terms have different meanings when used in connection with different media; in such cases, the definitions given are those used in regard to cable.

AA.   See *Average Audience.*

Access.   See *Leased Access, Public Access.*

ADI.   See *Area of Dominant Influence.*

Adjacency.   A commercial time period just before or just after a program as opposed to one occurring during the program itself.

Advertorial.   A commercial, usually over 30 seconds in length, in which an advertiser presents a commentary or editorial point of view on an issue rather than a sales or corporate image message. This term is often erroneously used to describe an infomercial.

Affidavit.   A document issued by a cable system or network attesting that a particular announcement or series of announcements has been run as ordered by the advertiser. It usually includes the time each announcement was run and the cost of each announcement.

157

Affiliate.   A cable system that has contracted to carry a network's programming.

Alphanumeric.   Literally, composed of alphabetic characters and/or numerals. Used in cable to describe material run on data channels.

Amplifier.   An electronic device that boosts or amplifies signals. Used in cable systems to maintain signal strength as signals are distributed throughout the system.

Announcement.   A message carried on a cable or broadcast outlet on behalf of an advertiser or public service organization.

Antenna.   A device used to intercept signals transmitted through the air by electromagnetic waves.

Antiope.   A teletext system developed in France.

Arbitron Ratings Company (ARB).   A national research firm engaged in radio, television, and cable audience measurement. Arbitron provides metered measurement of television audiences in 14 markets; other reports are based on diary samples.

Area of Dominant Influence (ADI).   Arbitron Ratings Company's geographic definition of a television market, specifically the counties in which the television stations in a metro area reach their largest audience (similar to A.C. Nielsen Company's Designated Market Area).

Audience.   A group of households or individuals exposed to a program or advertising message.

Audience Composition.   The classification of an audience into specific categories such as age, sex, income, and education.

Audience Duplication.   The number or percent of households reached by a particular program that are also reached by another program. For example, if a syndicated program appears on two different channels, the audience duplication would consist of those people who see it on both channels.

Audience Flow.   The change in audience during and between programs. This measures such items as tune-ins, tune-outs, and channel shifts.

Audience Profile.   The demographic characteristics of the individuals or households viewing a particular program or channel.

Avail.   See *Availability*.

Availability (Avail).   The commercial time a cable system or network has available for sale. Also refers to specific units of unsold time.

Average Audience (AA). The estimated average number of individuals or households viewing a program or channel during each minute of programming measured.

Average Episodes per Viewing Household/Person. The average number of quarter-hours of programming viewed by individuals or households reached.

Average Hours. The average number of hours of programming viewed by an individual or household over a specified period of time.

BAR. See *Broadcast Advertisers Reports.*

Barter. The exchange of advertising time in programming for merchandise or services. As an adjective, the term refers to syndicated programming supplied at little or no charge to a broadcaster or cablecaster because it comes inclusive of commercials presold by the producer.

B.A.S.I.C. See *Broadcast Advertising Schedules Impacted by Cable.*

Basic Cable. The program services distributed by a cable television system to subscribers for a basic monthly fee. These may include one or more of local broadcast stations, distant broadcast stations, nonpay cable networks, local origination programming, and/or data channels.

Bicycling. Distribution of programming and/or commercials between systems by sending tapes by mail or messenger service. (This term derives from the early practice of several movie theaters sharing the same film print having a messenger carry the print between theaters by bicycle in time for each to show the movie as scheduled.)

Billboard. A brief announcement, usually at the beginning and/or end of a program, naming the sponsor(s) or participating advertiser(s).

Bonus Spot. A free spot given to an advertiser either as an incentive to buy additional time (usually as part of a package buy) or a replacement for a commercial that did not run as scheduled. See *Make Good.*

BRC. See *Electronic Media Rating Council.*

Broadcast Advertisers Reports (BAR). A research service that reports on commercial activity and estimated advertising expenditures on cable, television, and radio.

Broadcast Advertising Schedules Impacted by Cable (B.A.S.I.C.).   A report combining Nielsen and BAR data to show audience delivery in cable and noncable households for all broadcast network television programming, broken out by advertiser and brand name.

Broadcasting.   The transmission of television or radio signals over the air for reception by the general public.

CAB.   See *Cabletelevision Advertising Bureau.*

Cable Audience Methodology Study.   Study conducted by the CAB/NCTA Research Standards Committee and the A.C. Nielsen Company to test proposed methodologies for measuring cable audiences more accurately than with standard television measurement techniques.

Cable On-Line Data Exchange.   An NHI on-line computerized service providing information on over 8,000 cable systems.

Cable Origination.   See *Cablecasting, Local Origination.*

Cable Penetration.   The percentage of homes within a given area that subscribe to cable.

Cable System.   See *Cable Television System.*

Cable System Operator.   The company or individual responsible for the operation of a cable television system (usually the system owner as well).

Cable Television Administration and Marketing Society (CTAM).   A professional society that deals with key management and marketing issues in the cable industry by providing a forum for idea exchange.

Cable Television System.   Commonly referred to as a *cable system.* A facility designed for the purpose of receiving multiple broadcast and/or nonbroadcast signals and distributing them via coaxial cable to subscribers living in unattached residences not under common ownership. Signals may be received over the air, by satellite or microwave relay, or from the system's studio or remote facilities.

Cablecasting.   An umbrella term referring to all material carried or generated for distribution on cable systems, excluding broadcast signals.

Cable-ready.   A term that describes television sets that have circuitry built in that enables them to receive and translate cable signals without the use of a separate converter. Cable-ready sets, however, usually cannot decode pay television signals that have been scrambled to prevent unauthorized reception.

Cabletelevision Advertising Bureau. A cable industry trade association whose purpose is to develop cable as an advertising medium by providing information to the advertising community and sales training and assistance to cable systems, networks, and sales representatives.

Cabletext. See *Teletext.*

CAMS. See *Cable Audience Methodology Study.*

CATA. See *Community Antenna Television Association.*

CATV. See *Community Antenna Television.*

CCI. See *Council for Cable Information.*

Channel Capacity. The number of channels available for current or future use on a cable system. Capacity is determined by the capabilities of the system hardware; actual offerings are determined by the cable company based on its own marketing decisions and any requirements specified in the franchise agreement.

Character Generator. A computer system that projects alphanumeric characters and electronic graphics on a television screen.

Circulation. The number of individuals or households tuned to a particular cable or broadcast signal during a specified period of time.

CLIO Awards. The advertising industry's equivalent of the Oscar, Emmy, or Tony awards for excellence. In 1982, award categories were introduced for network and local cable commercials.

Coaxial Cable. The medium used to carry cable signals between sources and destinations—for example, system headends and subscriber homes, downlinks and headends, studios and uplinks. It is made in various sizes to meet diverse use requirements, but basically consists of copper wire surrounded by insulating material often made of a foam plastic. There may be several concentric layers of wire and insulator within a single cable depending on what it is used for.

CODE. See *Cable On-Line Data Exchange.*

Coincidental Interview. A measurement technique in which an interviewer questions a respondent (by telephone or in person) about what the respondent is viewing on television at the time of the interview.

Commercial. An announcement paid for by an advertiser.

Community Antenna Television (CATV). One of the original terms for cable television, referring to its original and in many cases still primary function of providing a community with a link to a well-placed master antenna in order to enable or improve reception of clear television signals not otherwise receivable.

Community Antenna Television Association (CATA).   A trade association for independently owned and operated cable systems and MSOs with autonomously managed systems.

Compulsory License.   Provision of the Copyright Act of 1976 that allows cable systems to distribute programming signals to subscribers without having to negotiate royalty agreements with individual program copyright holders.

Converter.   A device that translates cable signals into television signals and allows the viewer to select individual channels.

Copyright Royalty Tribunal.   The regulatory body established under the Copyright Act of 1976 to determine the royalties to be paid to copyright holders for use of their copyrighted materials.

Co-sponsorship.   Sponsorship of a program by two or more advertisers.

Cost per Point (CPP).   The cost of running a commercial divided by the size of the viewing audience as expressed in rating points. For example, if a commercial cost $2,000 to run and received a viewership rating of 5, the cost per point would be $400 ($2,000/5). In media planning, the estimated cost of reaching 1 rating point of viewership in a particular program or daypart.

Cost per Thousand (CPM).   The cost of running a commercial divided by the size of the viewing audience as measured in groups of 1,000. For example, if a commercial cost $2,000 to run and was seen by 500,000 viewers, the cost per thousand would be $4 ($2,000/500). CPM is the most commonly used cost efficiency comparison measurement used in media planning.

Council for Cable Information.   A cable industry trade association established in 1983 to cultivate positive consumer attitudes toward cable as a unique beneficial service to the home and the community.

County Size.   A method of classifying counties (as A, B, C, or D) according to size and proximity to or content of metropolitan areas. See *Standard Metropolitan Statistical Area.*

CPM.   See *Cost per Thousand.*

CPP.   See *Cost per Point.*

Crawl.   A horizontally moving alphanumeric display. Vertical crawls are called *scrolls.*

CTAM.   See *Cable Television Administration and Marketing Society.*

Cume. See *Cumulative Audience.*

Cumulative Audience (Cume). The number of different (nonduplicated) people tuned to a cable or broadcast signal during a specified period of time. Also called *reach.*

Data Channels. An umbrella term for all forms of video transmission that involve electronically generated text and/or graphics rather than recorded or live action images. Generally refers to local cable channels on which alphanumeric material is displayed by character generators, although videotex and teletext also fall into this category.

DBS. See *Direct Broadcast Satellite.*

Decoder. A device used to unscramble scrambled signals or to decode teletext signals transmitted through the vertical blanking interval.

Dedicated Channel. A cable channel used to carry only programming from a single source, as opposed to *cherry-picking* from two or more sources.

Demographics. Measurements of audiences based on classifications of personal, social, or economic characteristics.

Designated Market Area (DMA). A.C. Nielsen Company's geographic definition of a television market, specifically the counties in which the television stations in a metro area reach their largest audience (similar to Arbitron Rating Company's Area of Dominant Influence).

Diary. An audience measurement technique in which individuals or households keep written records of their television viewing over a specified period of time (usually a week).

Direct Broadcast Satellite (DBS). A service that transmits satellite signals directly to a home through the viewer's own earth station rather than through a cable system.

Direct-Response Advertising. Advertising involving commercials, generally 120 seconds in length, from which the viewer can order the product or service being advertised by calling a toll-free number or writing to a particular address, usually a post office box. See also *Per-Inquiry Advertising.*

Dish. A colloquial term for a convex disc-shaped satellite antenna (some people use it for satellite antennas in general).

Distant Signal. A broadcast signal originating outside the cable system's local market as defined by the FCC under the mandatory carriage rule.

Distribution System. The part of the cable system that carries signals from the system headend to the home, including the coaxial cable, amplifiers, and drops.

Downlink. The transmission of a signal from a satellite to an earth station, and the hardware involved in the process.

Downstream. The direction signals sent from the cable system headend to subscriber homes are said to travel.

Drop. The connection between a cable system's feeder line and a subscriber's television set. A *drop box* connected to the feeder line allows installers to attach *drop cables,* which are strung from the box to the subscriber's home and connected to the converter on each set.

Earth Station. An installation used to transmit signals to and/or receive signals from satellites. Most earth stations used by cable systems are *TVRO (television receiving only)*; they pick up signals from a satellite and relay them to the cable system headend. TVRO stations include one or more satellite antennas (usually shaped as concave discs 4 to 10 meters in diameter, although also made in horn and parabolic configurations) and signal reception and amplification equipment.

Efficiency. The comparative value of a spot measured against other spots using such criteria as **CPM** or **CPP.** Greater efficiency may be defined as larger audience for the same amount of money, or conversely, less money for the same audience.

Electronic Media Rating Council (EMRC). Founded in 1964 as the Broadcast Rating Council (BRC), expanded to become the EMRC in 1982. An independent organization of electronic media research users formed to develop standards for, and audit compliance with them by, syndicated audience measurement services.

EMRC. See *Electronic Media Rating Council.*

Fiber Optics. A method of transmitting signals over light waves sent through extremely thin fibers spun from glass. Fiber optic cables can carry greater amounts of information than copper wire carrying electrical signals.

Flighting. A method of scheduling commercials so that they run at various separate times within a broad period rather than continuously.

Footprint. The geographic area within which a satellite-relayed signal can be received.

Fragmentation. The division of an audience due to the introduction of additional programming sources or other alternatives.

Franchise; Franchise Agreement.   A contract between a cable television company and a municipal government authorizing the company to and defining the terms under which it may install coaxial cable and offer cable television service within the community.

Franchise Area.   The specific geographic area in which the cable television company may offer service, as defined by the franchise.

Frequency.   The average number of times an individual or household viewed a particular program, channel, or commercial over a specified period of time. It is calculated by dividing GRP by the cume.

Frequency Distribution.   The number of individuals or households that viewed a particular program, channel, or commercial over a specified period of time, broken out by the number of times viewed.

Geosynchronous Orbit.   An orbital path 22,300 miles above the earth where a satellite's velocity in relation to the earth's rotation is such that the satellite continuously remains above a specific geographic point. Also called *geostationery orbit.*

Gross Audience.   The total number of individuals or households viewing two or more spots or programs, without taking into account any audience duplication.

Gross Impressions.   Gross rating points projected to actual audiences.

Gross Rating Points (GRP).   The sum of all rating points achieved for a particular period of time.

GRP.   See *Gross Rating Points.*

Headend.   The equipment at a cable system which receives the various program source signals, processes them, and retransmits them to subscribers.

Homes Passed.   The number of homes in which cable television service is or can be readily made available because feeder cables are in place nearby.

Households Using Television (HUT).   The total number of households in which at least one person is viewing television on one or more sets during a specified period of time. Some people have suggested that cable should also be measured in terms of *Households Using Cable Television (HUCT).*

HUT.   See *Households Using Television.*

Independent Station.   A broadcast television station not affiliated with any of the three major broadcast television networks. (The FCC definition includes stations offering less than 10 hours a week of network programming.)

Infomercial.   A commercial, usually 90 seconds or more in length, designed to supply information about a product or service, or about a topic relating to the advertiser's product or service, rather than to present a specific sales message.

Interactive Cable.   Cable systems that have the technical ability to let subscribers communicate directly with a computer at the system headend from their television sets, using special converters and the regular cable lines.

Interconnect.   Two or more cable systems distributing a programming signal simultaneously, primarily to maximize the effectiveness of an advertising schedule by offering a multiple system buy in which only one contract need be negotiated. Interconnects can be *hard,* where systems are directly linked by cable or by microwave relays and the signal is fed to the entire interconnect by one headend, or *soft,* where there is no direct operational connection between the participating systems but the same commercial is run simultaneously by each of the systems.

Leased Access.   On some systems, a public access channel for which programmers pay a nominal fee for use and are thereby permitted to sell commercial time in their programming.

Leased Channel.   A channel on a cable system which the system has leased to a third party for that party's use. The lessor, not the cable system, is responsible for the programming on the channel.

Lift.   The increase in basic cable penetration brought about by the introduction of a new programming service.

Local Origination Programming.   Programming produced by or under the auspices of a local cable system for presentation on the system. It may also include syndicated programming acquired by the system for presentation thereon.

Make Good.   A commercial announcement run by a cable system or network for an advertiser to compensate for a spot that did not run as scheduled or was run improperly.

Mandatory Carriage.   The FCC rule requiring cable systems to carry all local broadcast television signals in their market. Also, the stations carried under the rule, commonly called *must-carries.*

Master Antenna Television (MATV).   An arrangement whereby a single antenna is used to provide television service for all units in a hotel, apartment house, or other housing complex. See also *Satellite Master Antenna Television.*

MATV.   See *Master Antenna Television.*

MDS. See *Multipoint Distribution System.*

Measurement Techniques. Methods used to determine media audiences. The most commonly used techniques are meters, diaries, and telephone coincidental interviews (see separate listings for each).

Meter. An electronic device which, when attached to a television set, records when the set is on and to what channel(s) it is tuned. Late-model meters store this information internally and can be accessed by telephone for collection of the data.

Metro Area. An area within a television market usually consisting of the counties falling within a Standard Metropolitan Statistical Area (SMSA). A metro area may be different from an SMSA due to adjustments for marketing considerations and historical usage, or in the absence of an SMSA may be separately defined using similar guidelines.

Metro Rating. A rating measured within a metro area.

Metro Share. A share measured within a metro area.

Microwave. A radio frequency of greater than 500 MHz used for short-range, line-of-sight communications.

Microwave Relay System. A system for picking up and retransmitting microwave signals. Since microwaves travel only in straight lines over short distances, relay systems are used to carry signals over longer distances—for example, for importing distant broadcast signals or for hard interconnects, or through areas where there are many obstacles (buildings, hills) between the origin point and the destination.

MSO. See *Multiple System Operator.*

Multiple System Operator (MSO). A company that owns and/or operates more than one cable system.

Multipoint Distribution System (MDS). A common carrier system that transmits microwave signals short distances within limited areas. Special antennas and converters are required in order to receive the signals. It is used in business for facsimile and data transmission; for consumer purposes, it is used to supply cable or other nonbroadcast programming services to areas not yet wired for cable.

Multiset Household. A household with more than one television set.

Must-carry. See *Mandatory Carriage.*

Narrowcasting. Programming designed to reach a specific group defined by demographics and/or program content.

National Cable Television Association (NCTA). A cable industry trade association dealing with public policy issues, programming, marketing, engineering, and operational aspects of the industry.

NCTA. See *National Cable Television Association.*

Network. A programming service that distributes its programming to affiliated cable systems, usually by satellite or microwave relay (sometimes by telephone lines or cable), for simultaneous transmission to subscribers. Also, as a group, the affiliated systems of the programming service.

A.C. Nielsen Company. An international business services company offering marketing and media research and other services best known for its television audience measurement services, which provide audience estimates for national television networks, local television stations, and cable programming services.

Nielsen Homevideo Index (NHI). The division of Nielsen's Media Research Group that measures cable, pay cable, home video, and related technology using NSI and NTI resources and methodologies. It is also responsible for developing new techniques to improve the measurement of these media.

Nielsen Station Index (NSI). The Nielsen rating service that measures the audiences of individual television stations on a local market basis in each DMA using the diary method. It also uses a meter sample in five major markets to provide overnight household ratings.

Nielsen Television Index (NTI). The Nielsen rating service that provides national audience estimates for broadcast and cable networks using a sample of metered households. It uses a separate diary home sample to provide age/sex audience composition data supplementing the meter-based estimates.

Nonduplication Rule. An FCC rule that prohibits cable systems from importing distant broadcast signals if they duplicate programming aired by local stations (in essence avoiding carriage of network programming from affiliates in different markets on the same system.)

Pay Cable. Cable programming services for which subscribers pay an additional fee above the basic cable service charge.

Pay-per-View. Pay television programming for which viewers pay a separate fee for each program viewed.

Pay Saturation. The proportion of homes subscribing to pay television measured as a percentage of (a) total homes passed and (b) total cable homes in a specified area.

Pay Television.   An umbrella term encompassing all television programming for which viewers pay a fee other than a basic cable
service charge, including pay cable, subscription television, and
multipoint distribution systems (see separate listing for each).

Penetration.   In cable, the proportion of homes subscribing to cable
measured as a percentage of the total number of homes in a
specified area.

Per-Inquiry Advertising.   Direct-response advertising for which the
cable network or system running the commercial is paid based on
the number of responses received rather than the commercial time
used.

Persons Using Television (PUT).   The total number of individuals
viewing television during a specified period of time.

Potential Audience.   The total audience (households or persons)
viewing television at a specified time and therefore theoretically
capable of viewing a particular program, channel, or commercial.

Prestel.   A teletext system developed and used in Great Britain.

Prime Time.   Peak evening television viewing hours, defined as 8 to 11
P.M. ET Monday–Saturday, 7 to 11 P.M. ET Sunday.

Projected Audience.   An audience estimate determined by applying
ratings to a universe estimate.

Public Access.   A noncommercial channel set aside by a cable system
for use by the public on a first-come, first-served nondiscriminatory
basis.

Quarter-Hour Audience.   The number of individuals watching a
particular program or channel for at least 6 minutes within a
specified 15-minute period.

QUBE.   Warner Amex Cable Communications' trade name for its
interactive cable hardware and service, often erroneously used to
refer to interactive cable in general.

Rating.   The percentage of *all* television households or of *all* people
within a demographic group in a survey area who view a
particular program or channel at a specified time.

Reach.   See *Cumulative Audience.*

ROS.   See *Run of Schedule.*

Run of Schedule (ROS).   The placement of an announcement in the
program schedule by a network or system at its discretion (though
sometimes within a contractually defined period), as opposed to
fixed position, where the advertiser specifies when its commercial
is to run.

Satcom.   A series of satellites owned and operated by RCA Americom, transponders on which many cable networks use to distribute their programming to cable systems.

Satellite; Communications Satellite.   A device placed in orbit around the earth that contains transponders which receive signals from particular points on earth and retransmit them over a wide geographic area. For cable purposes, it is used to distribute network programming to cable systems.

Satellite Master Antenna Television (SMATV).   The same as master antenna television (see separate listing), except that the antenna used is one for satellite signals rather than for over-the-air signals.

Scatter Plan.   An advertising media purchase plan in which the commercials are spread over a wide variety of times and programming so as to diversify and broaden the reach of the advertising.

Scrambler.   A device used to distort transmitted signals so that they cannot be viewed without the use of a decoding device at the receiving end. It is used by cable systems and networks to frustrate unauthorized reception of programming by nonsubscribing viewers.

Share (Share of Audience).   The percentage of households using television viewing a particular program or channel at a specified time.

Signal Carriage.   The broadcast stations, local or distant, carried on a cable system.

Signal Importation.   Carriage by a cable system of distant broadcast signals, usually by use of microwave relay systems.

SMATV.   See *Satellite Master Antenna Television.*

SMSA.   See *Standard Metropolitan Statistical Area.*

Spot.   Literally, a unit of commercial time available for sale by a cable system to a local advertiser (*local spot*) or a national advertiser (*national spot*). Colloquially used as a synonym for commercial.

SRDS.   See *Standard Rate and Data Service.*

Standard Metropolitan Statistical Area.   An area defined by the U.S. Office of Management and Budget as including a city with population of 50,000 or more, the county in which it is located, and any contiguous counties of a metropolitan character which are socioeconomically integrated with the central county.

Standard Rate and Data Service (SRDS).   A leading publisher of directories of advertising rates for broadcast and print media and of co-op advertising plans.

STV.   See *Subscription Television.*

Subscriber.   A household or business that legally receives and pays for cable and/or pay television service for its own use (not for retransmission).

Subscription Television (STV).   A broadcast (not cable) television service for which subscribers pay a monthly fee. The signals are transmitted scrambled, and subscribers are given decoders for their television sets.

Superstation.   This term properly refers only to television station WTBS in Atlanta, though it is now generically used to describe any broadcast television station that has its signal distributed nationally by satellite.

Survey Area.   The geographic area from which a study sample is drawn.

Tag.   Information verbally announced at and/or visually superimposed over the end of a commercial. The intent is to give additional or clarifying information relating to the commercial, such as the names of stores where a product may be purchased or announcement of a special promotion.

Target Audience.   The audience or portion thereof that an advertiser considers the most likely and/or desired prospects for a product, service, or message.

Teletext.   Alphanumeric material transmitted to and displayed on television sets equipped with suitable decoding equipment. *Broadcast teletext* refers to teletext sent over the air; *cable teletext,* sometimes called *cabletext,* refers to teletext transmitted by cable or satellite to cable systems.

Telidon.   An alphageometric teletext system developed and used in Canada.

Tiering.   Supplying subscribers to a cable system with one or more programming services beyond the basic offerings at an extra charge. Each additional price increment, or the service(s) offered therefor, is called a *tier.*

Transponder.   A device on a satellite that receives signals and retransmits them.

TVRO.   See *Earth Station.*

Two-Way Cable.   Literally, coaxial cable capable of carrying signals in two directions, such as from the subscriber home to the system headend as well as vice versa. Colloquially, this term is frequently used in place of interactive cable.

Universe.   The population chosen for a study, from which a sample is drawn for testing and to which the test results are projected.

Uplink.   The transmission of a signal from an earth station to a satellite, and the hardware involved in the process.

Upstream.   The direction signals sent from subscriber homes to the cable system headend are said to travel (applicable to interactive cable systems only).

Vertical Blanking Interval.   The portion of the television signal that defines the screen image boundaries. It is also used to carry teletext and captioning signals.

Videotex.   A system for transmitting alphanumeric and/or graphic material to subscribers that allows direct interaction between the viewer and the originating service by use of a computer terminal.

Westar.   A series of satellites owned and operated by Western Union, transponders on which some cable networks use to distribute their programming to cable systems.

AFTERWORD

One of the nice things about the cable advertising business, I have found, is the willingness (and often, eagerness) of people to share their ideas and experiences with others in the field.

If you have success stories (or not-quite-success stories), creative ideas, or other comments or suggestions you would like to pass along for possible use in future editions of this book, I would like to hear about them. Letters and videotapes (¾-inch, please) may be sent to me at:

Zachary Associates
29 Harvard Lane
Hastings-on-Hudson, NY 10706

INDEXES

GENERAL INDEX

INDEX OF ADVERTISERS, ADVERTISING AGENCIES, AND PRODUCT CATEGORIES

INDEX OF CABLE COMPANIES AND SERVICES